I0468755

Come, Color My Garden

30 Grayscale images for you to COLOR the ARTIST'S WAY

Adult coloring books have been embraced by so many as a stress-relieving activity. Coloring as an adult can remind us of the simpler days of childhood. Maybe it's time for you to recapture a childhood pleasure.

I've taken photographs of my favorite flowers, shrubs, trees & all things 'garden'. This book contains **30** grayscale images made from my color photographs from my own yard & gardens.

Many adult coloring books contain line drawings, as did most of those we used in childhood, but I wanted to contribute to art education by showing you the gradations of color in the way artists think about their drawings & paintings.

As an artist, I create a 'value' sketch in black & white to show me where the darks & lights are. I then know where to paint in deeper colors the areas requiring the depth of color to create two dimensional painting that seems more realistic.

I find that the grayscale images are particularly lovely when I use colored pencils. Applied over the darker parts of the images, they bring richness & depth. I sometimes soften edges using pastels. Color crayons are good too. YOU are the artist here! You get to choose what coloring implements you enjoy.

NOTE:
If you use gel pens, felt tips, or other more 'liquid' mediums, please put a piece of cardstock or other paper behind your color work to catch any 'bleed through'. Please remember that my images are for your personal use only. You don't have permission to sell, distribute or reproduce them in any form.

~ *Janet Long Arts* ~

ETSY https://www.janetlongarts/shop/Etsy.com

WEBSITE [under construction]   www.janetlongarts.com

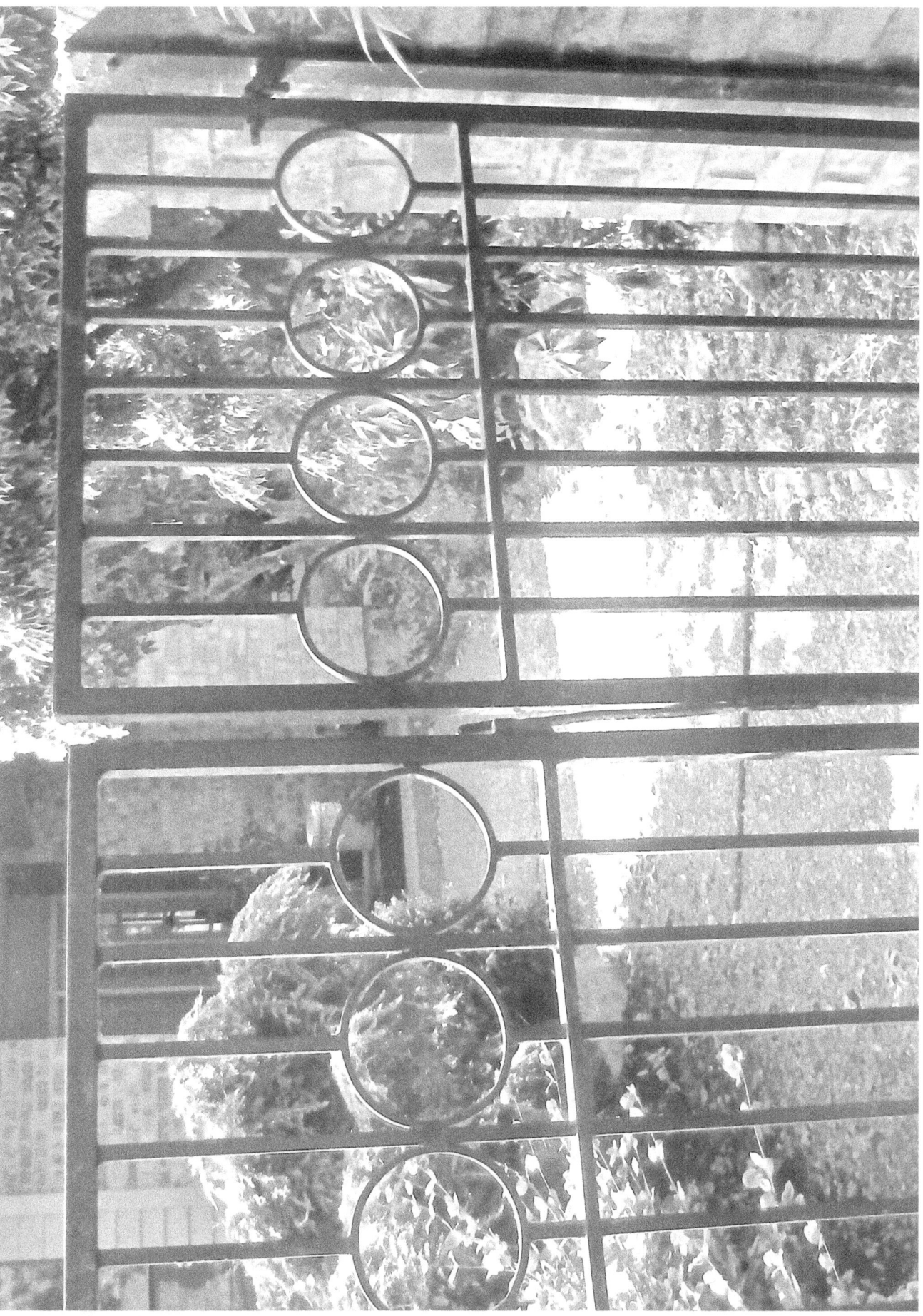

~ Garden Gate ~

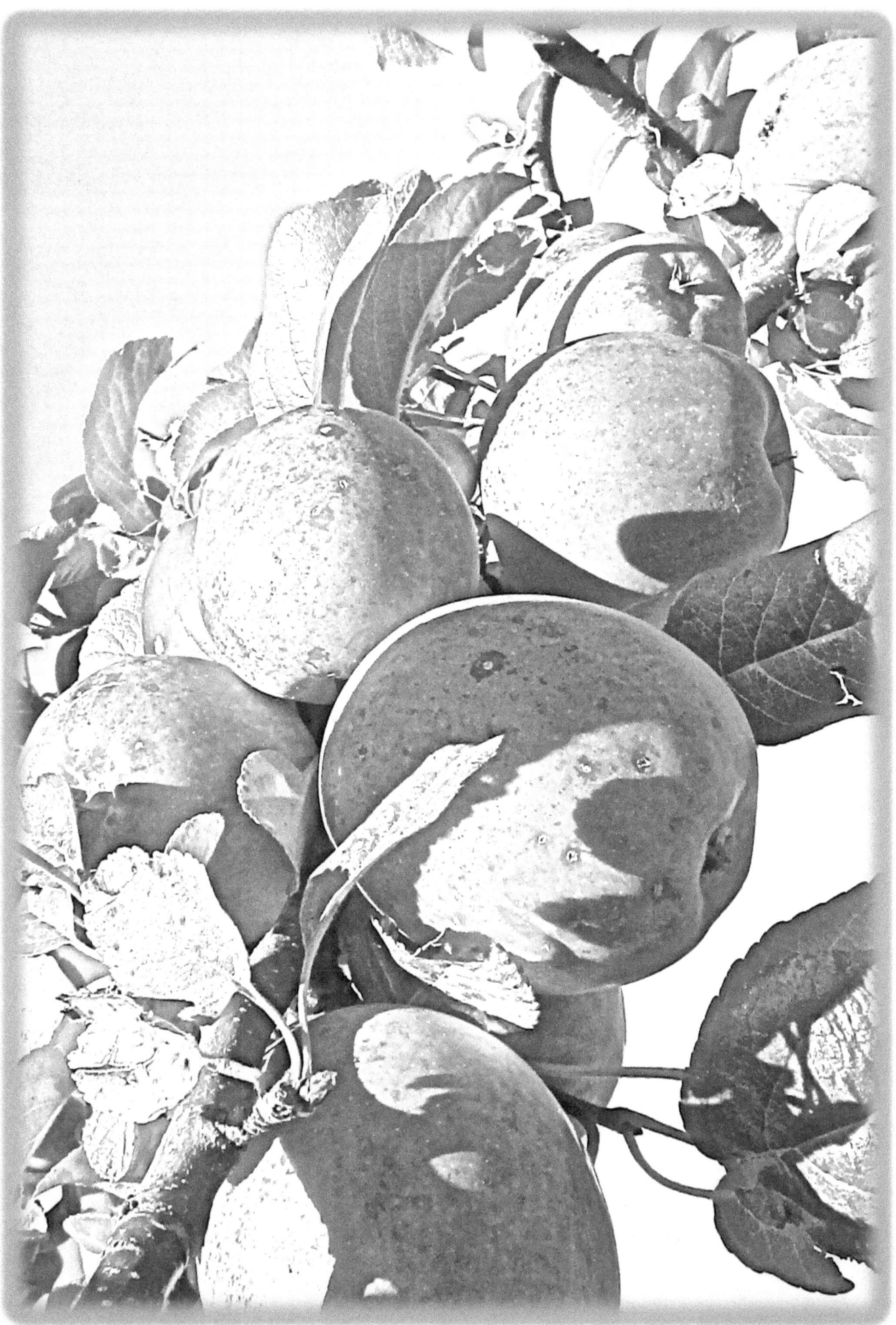

~ *Apples* ~

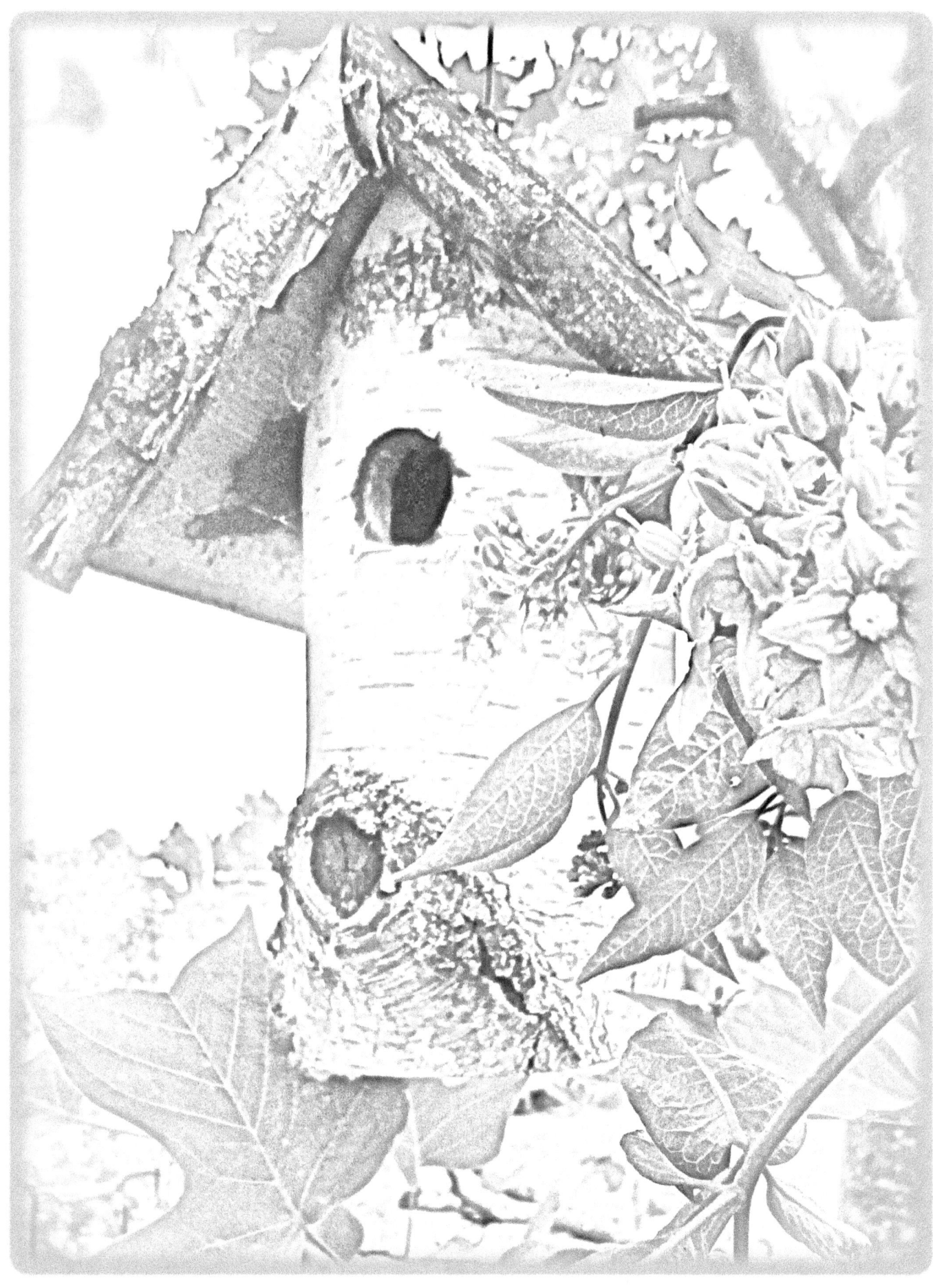

~ *Spring Birdhouse* ~

ETSY https://www.janetlongarts/shop/Etsy.com

WEBSITE [under construction] www.janetlongarts.com

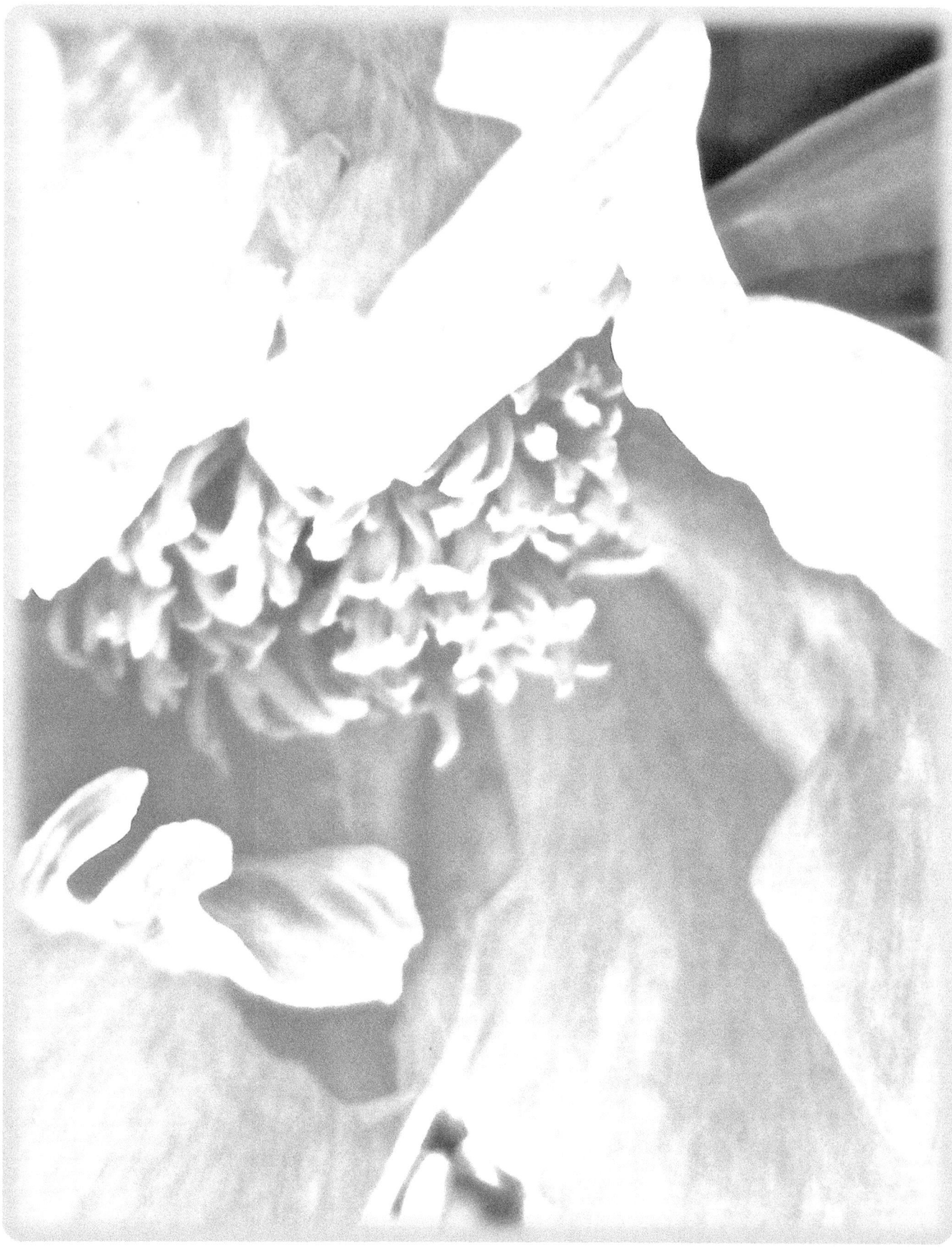

~ *Peony "Fire"* ~

ETSY https://www.janetlongarts/shop/Etsy.com

WEBSITE [under construction] www.janetlongarts.com

The right to reproduce does not transfer with sale of artwork.

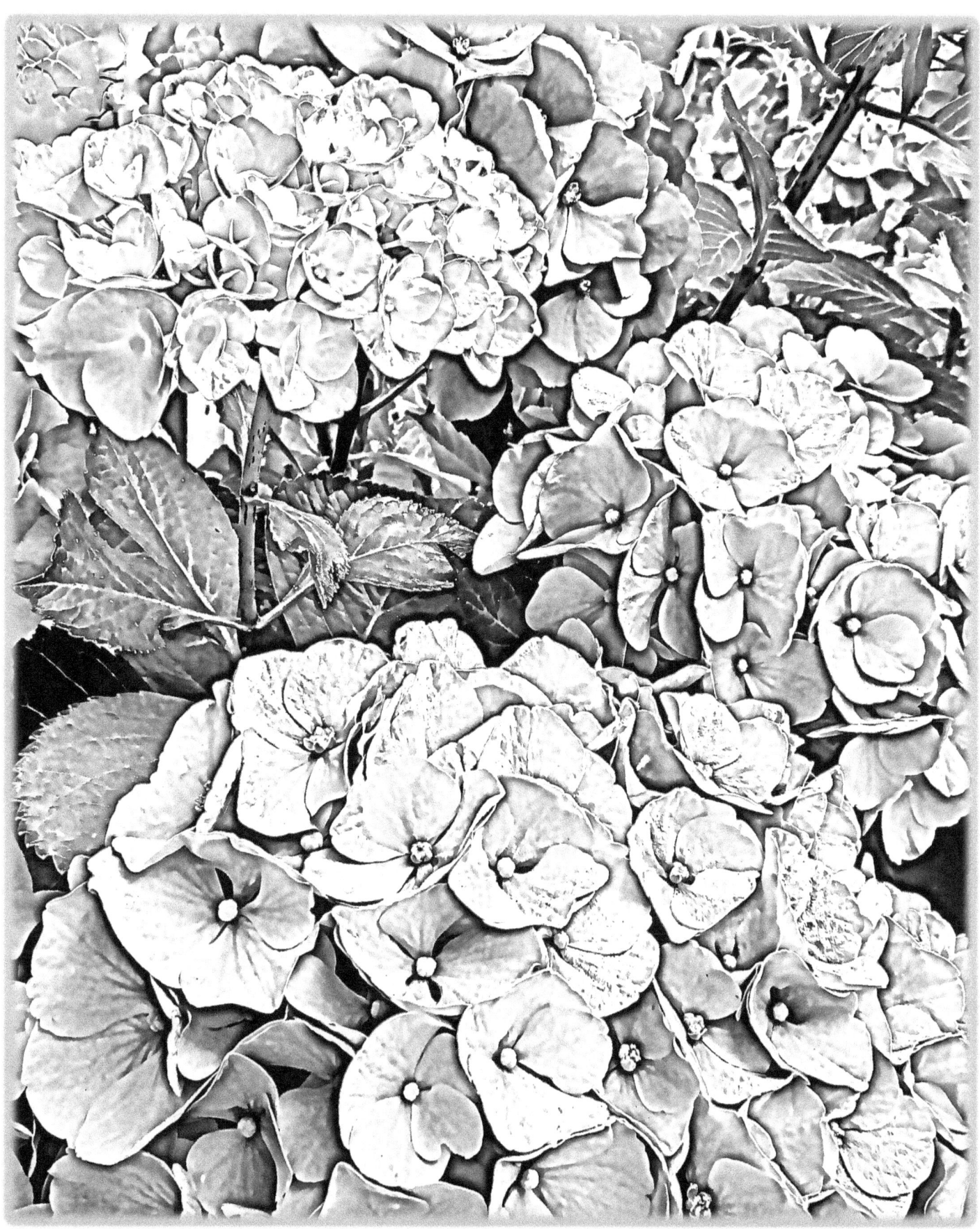

~ *Hydrangea* ~

ETSY https://www.janetlongarts/shop/Etsy.com

WEBSITE [under construction] www.janetlongarts.com

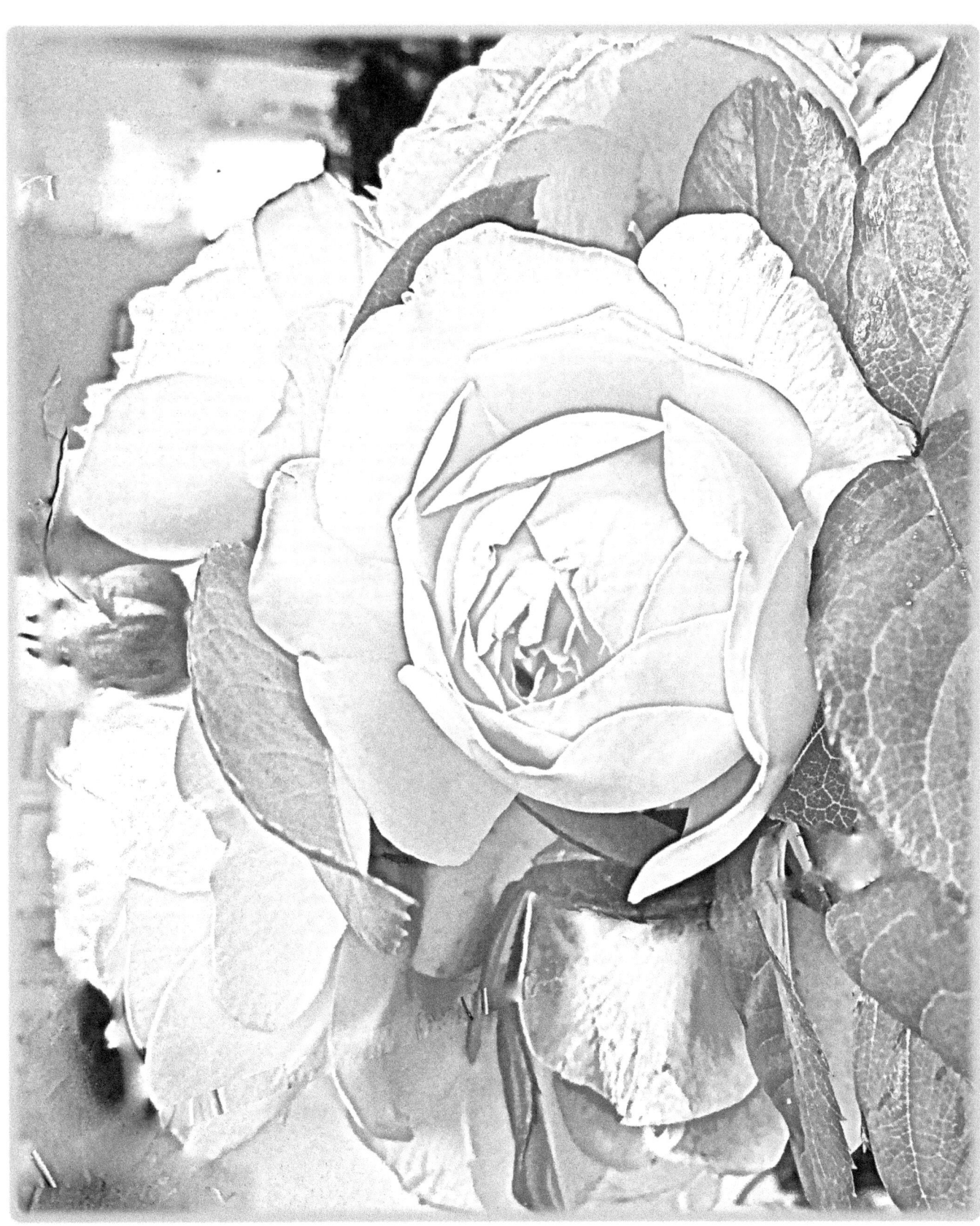

~ Graham Stuart Thomas Rose ~

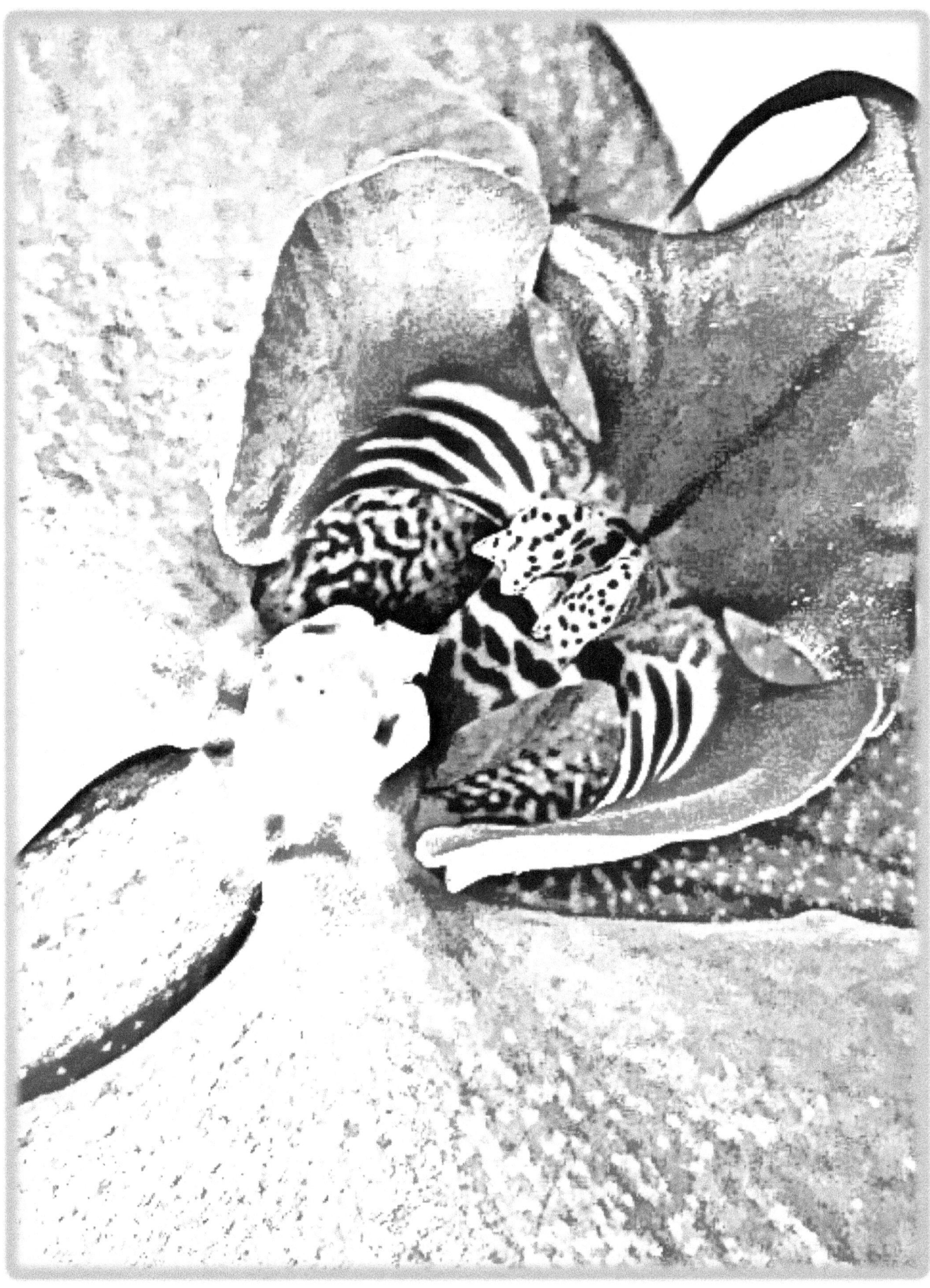

~ *Kitchen Orchid* ~

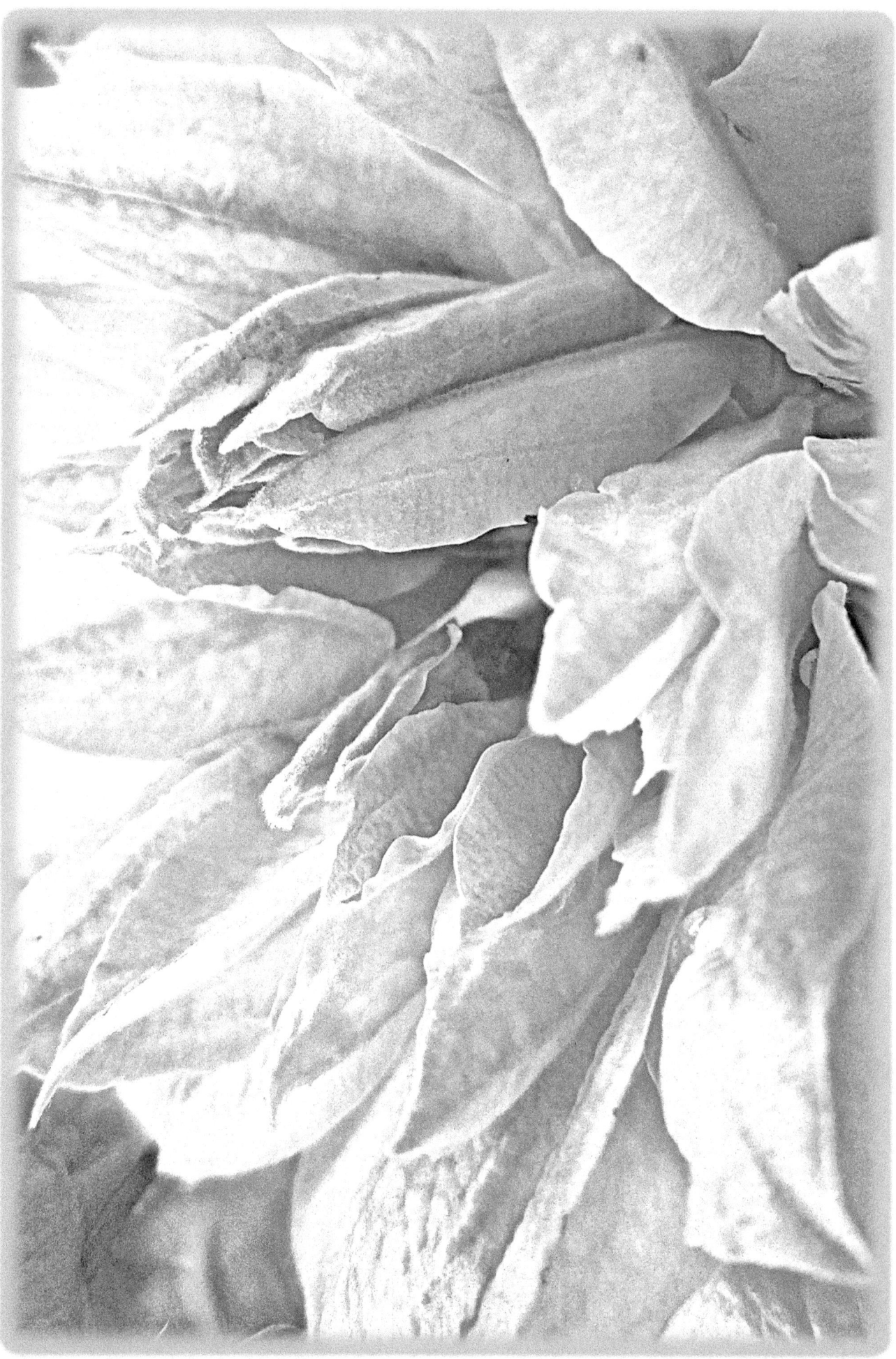

~ "TEA" Clematis ~
(Turquoise, Emerald, Amethyst are original colors)
ETSY https://www.janetlongarts/shop/Etsy.com
WEBSITE [under construction] www.janetlongarts.com
The right to reproduce does not transfer with sale of artwork.

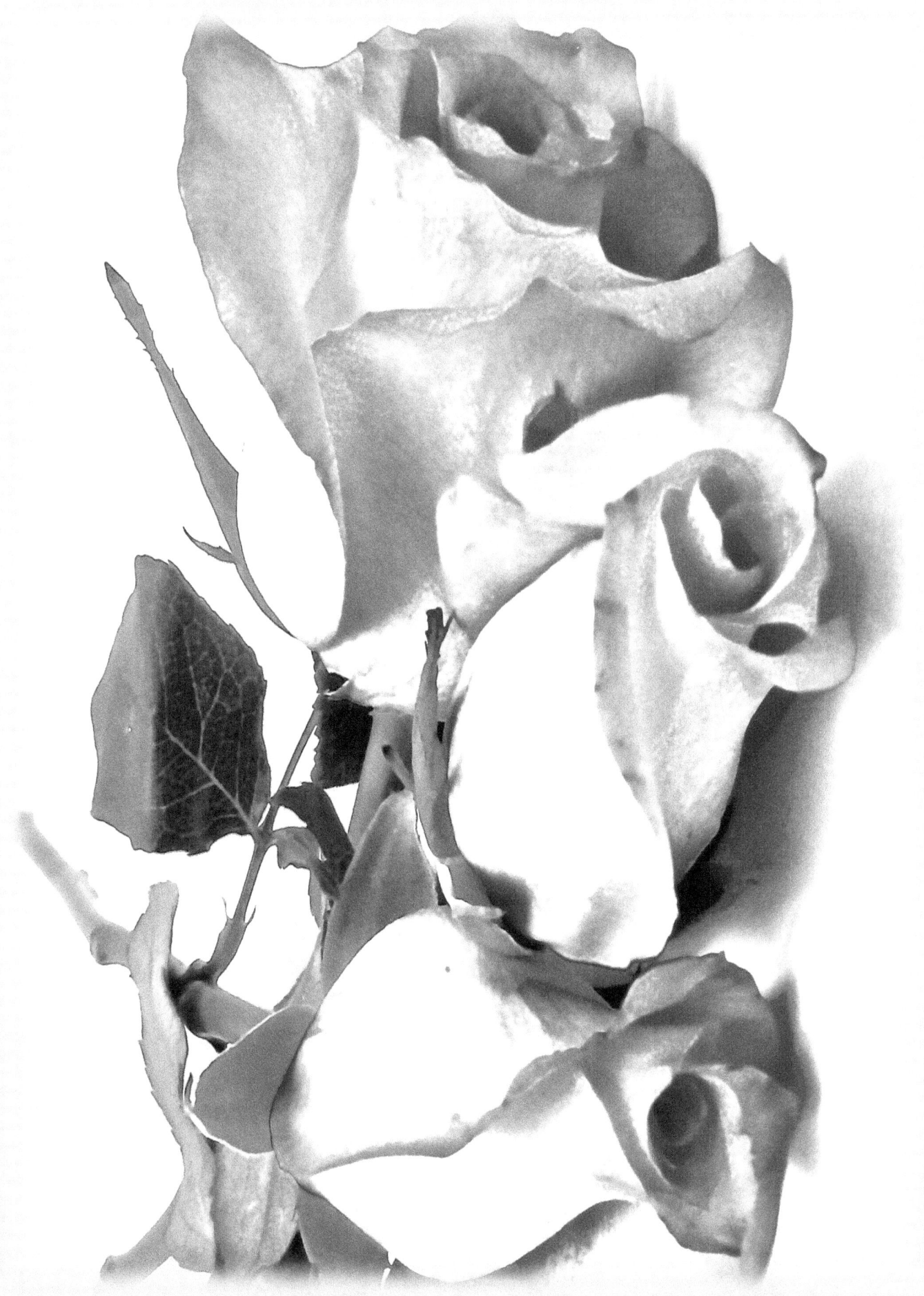

~ *Rose Bouquet* ~

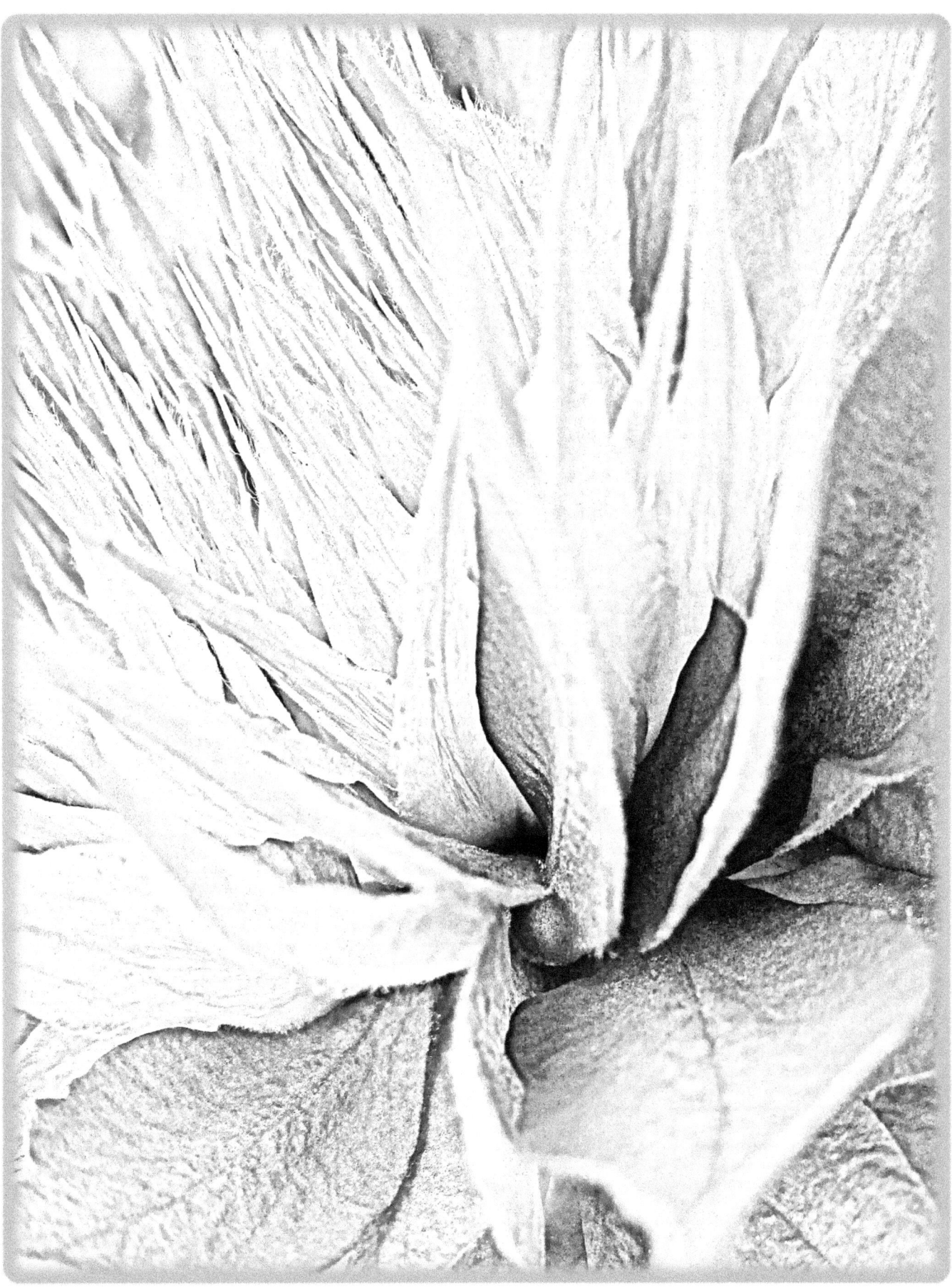

~ Josephine Clematis ~

ETSY https://www.janetlongarts/shop/Etsy.com

WEBSITE [under construction]   www.janetlongarts.com

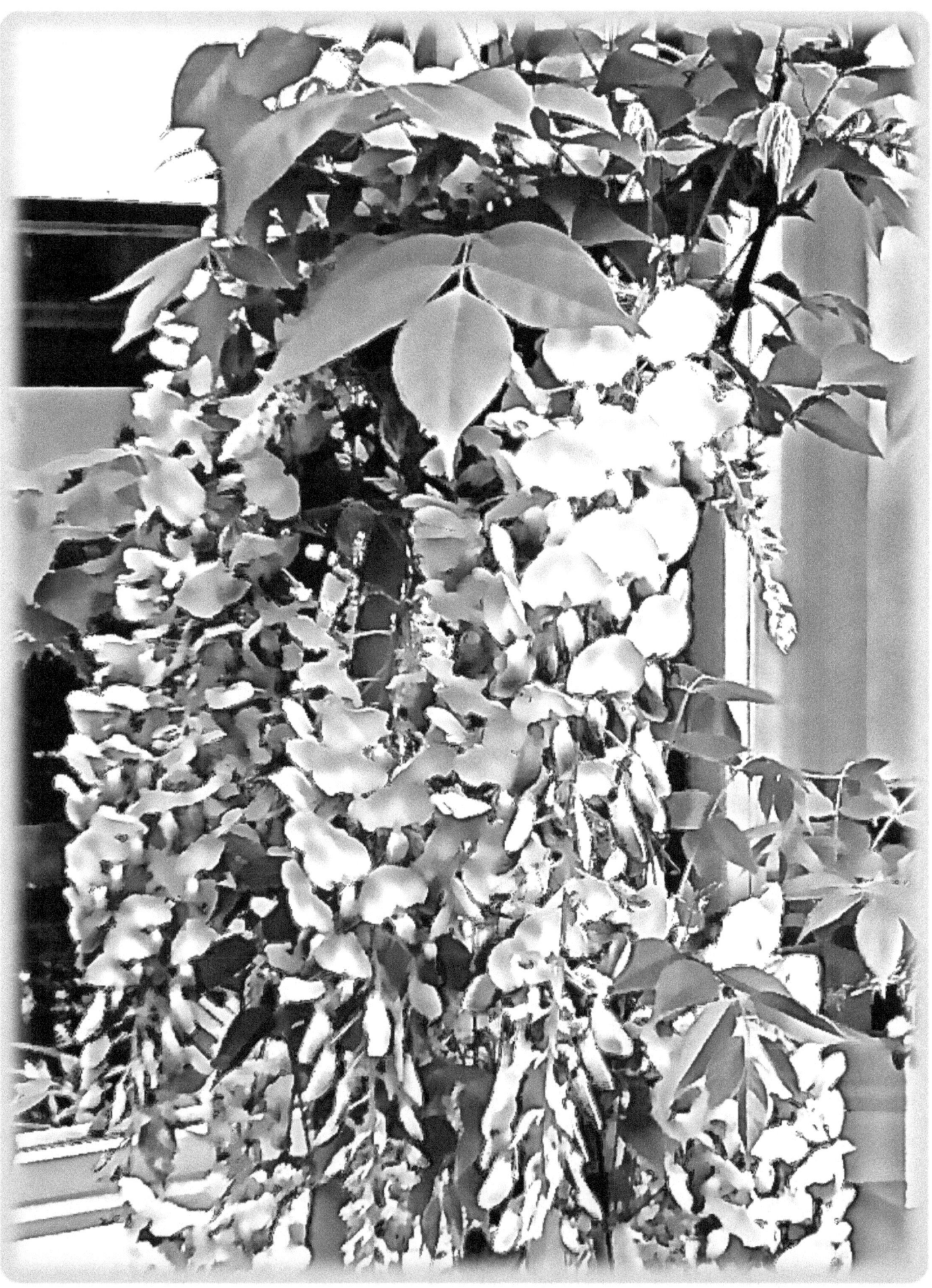

~ "Bill" Wisteria ~

ETSY https://www.janetlongarts/shop/Etsy.com

WEBSITE [under construction] www.janetlongarts.com

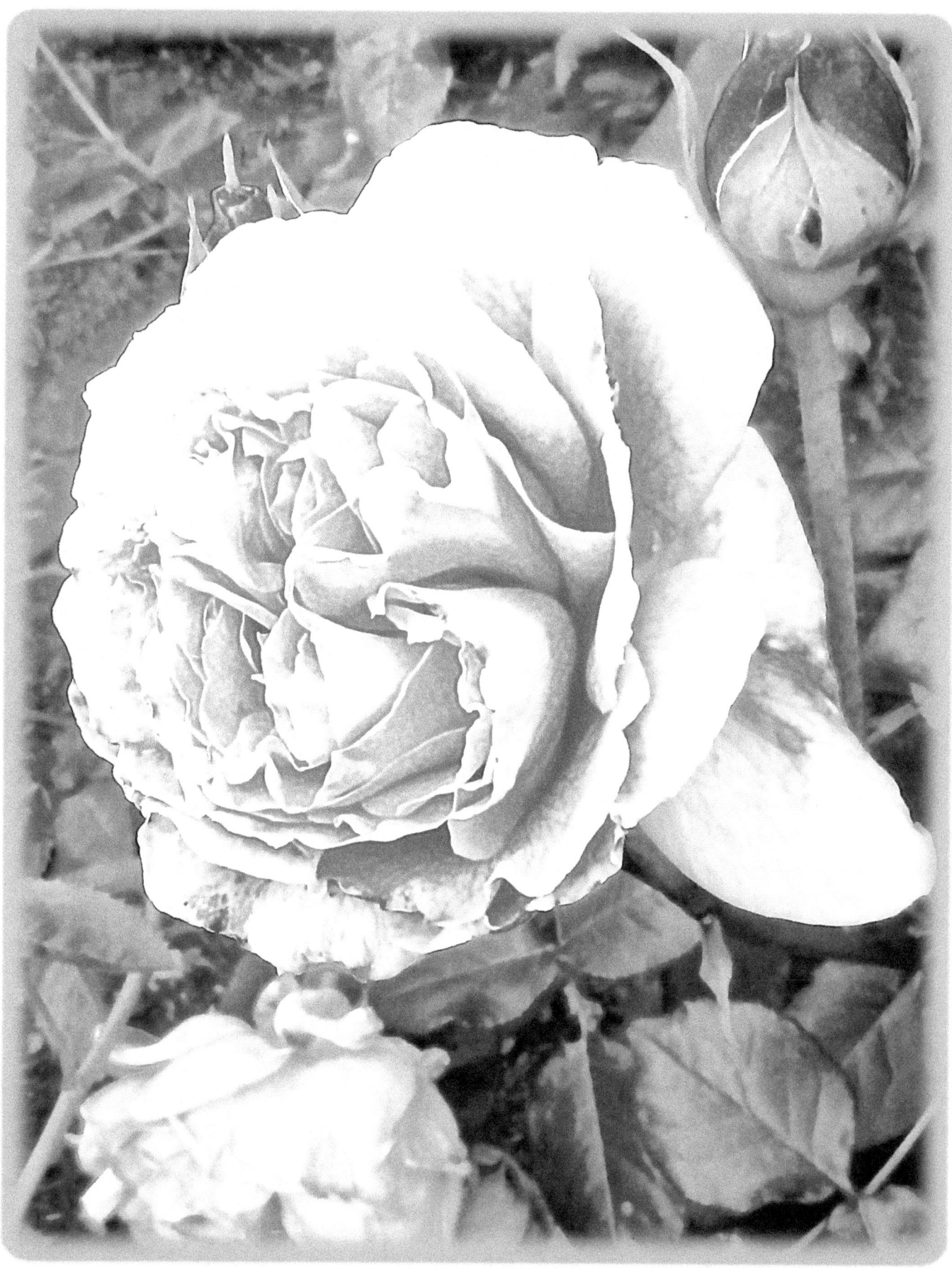

~ Abraham Darby ~

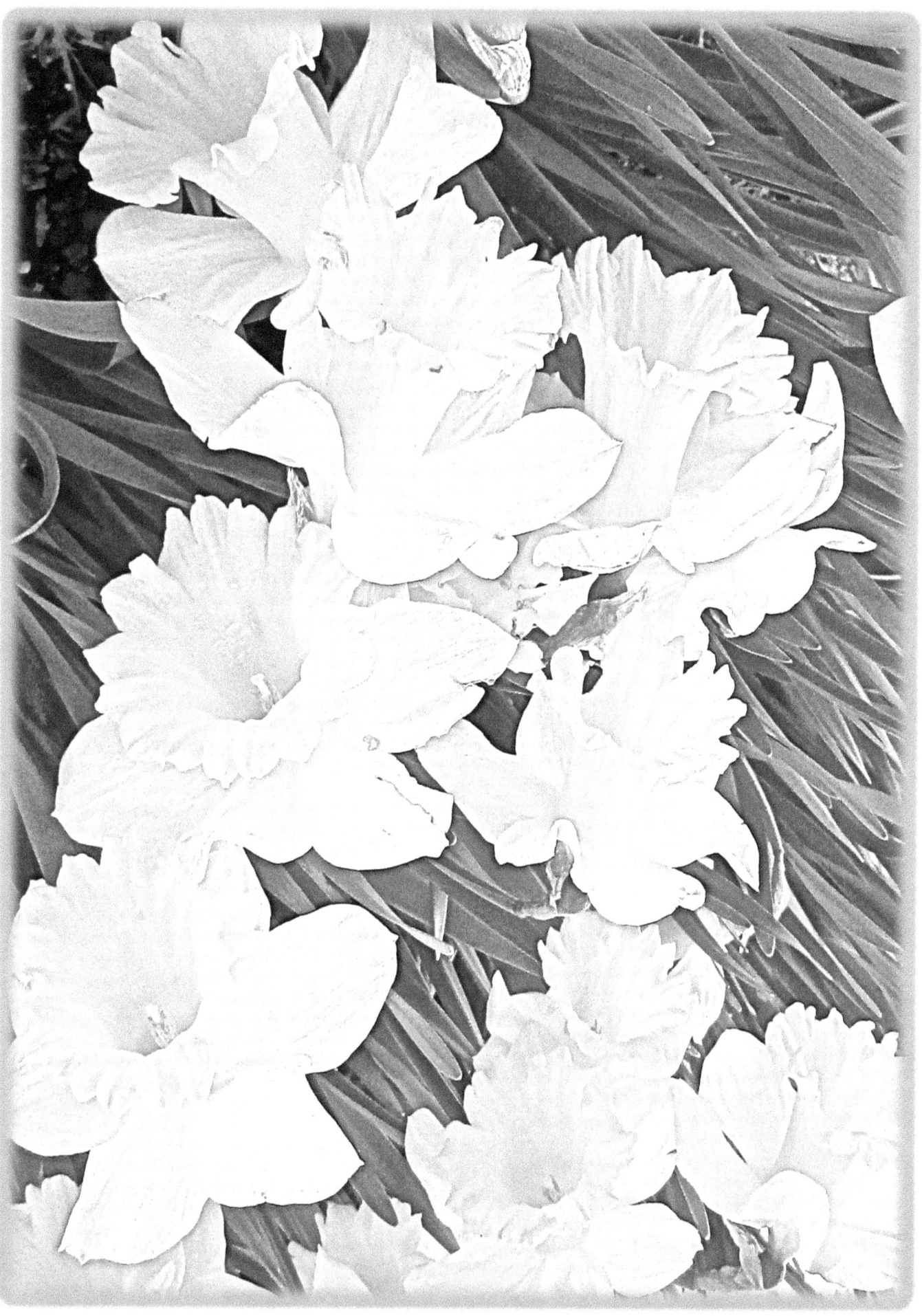

~ *Daffodils* ~

ETSY https://www.janetlongarts/shop/Etsy.com

WEBSITE [under construction] www.janetlongarts.com

The right to reproduce does not transfer with sale of artwork.

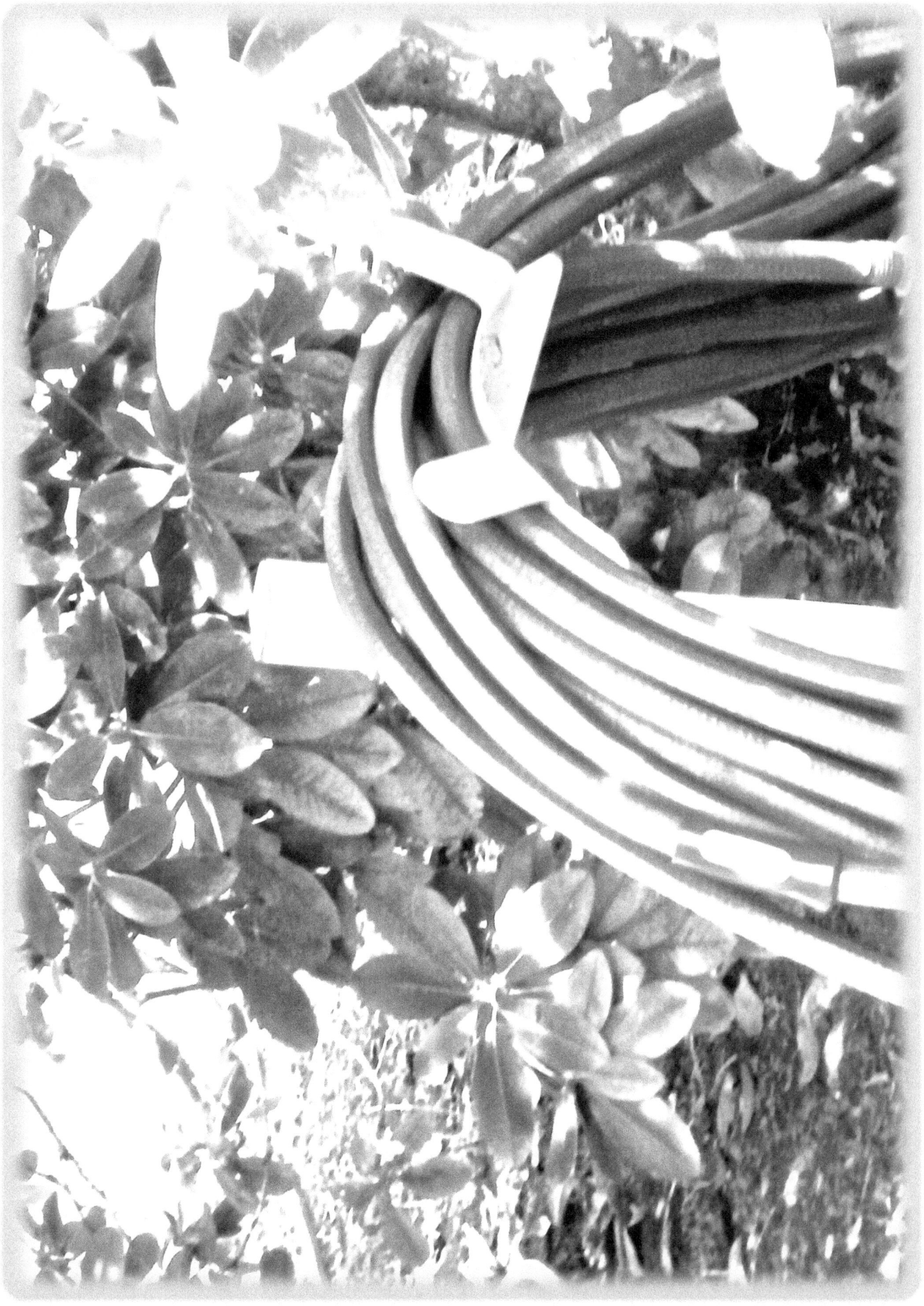

~ Garden Hose ~

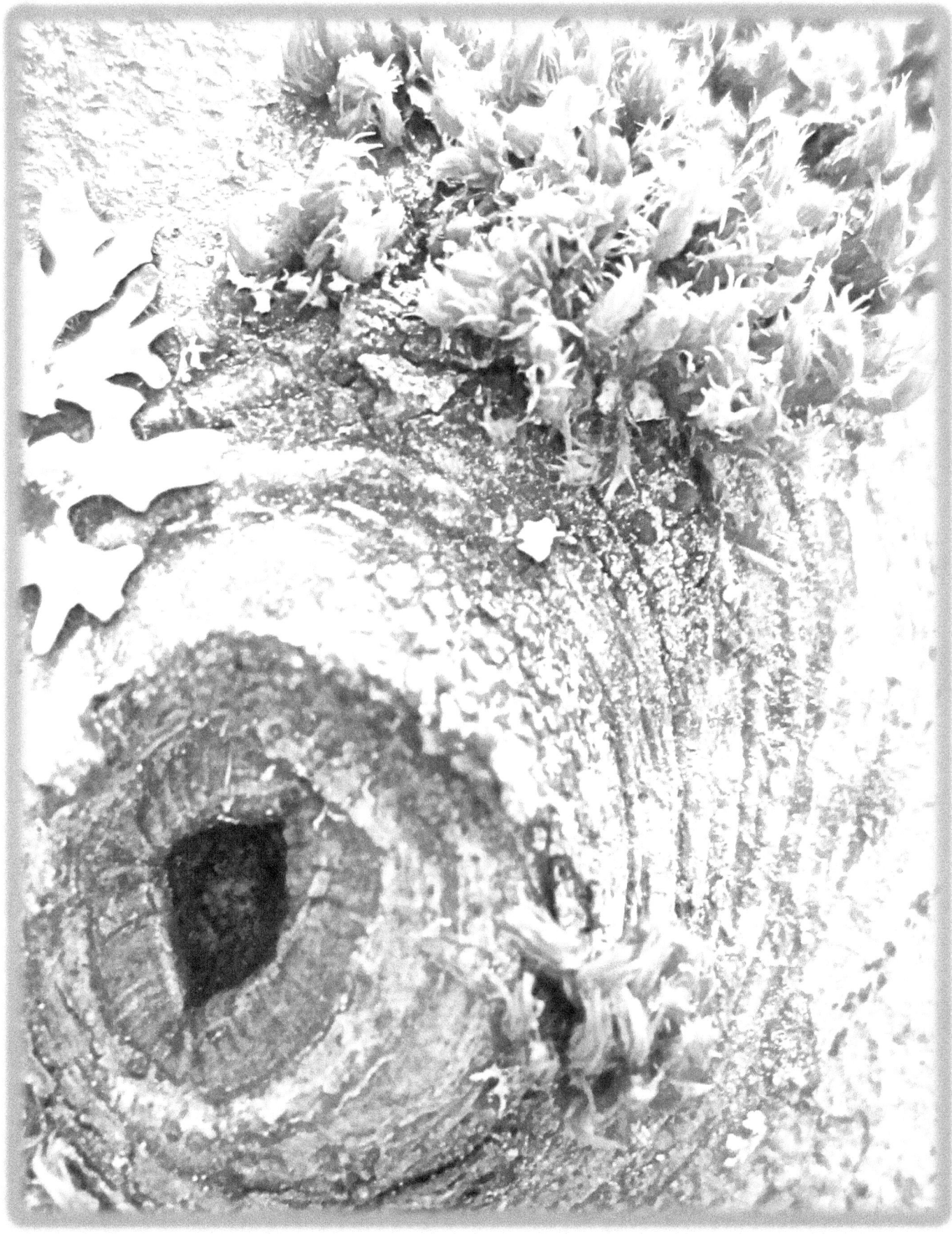

~ *Mossy Maple* ~

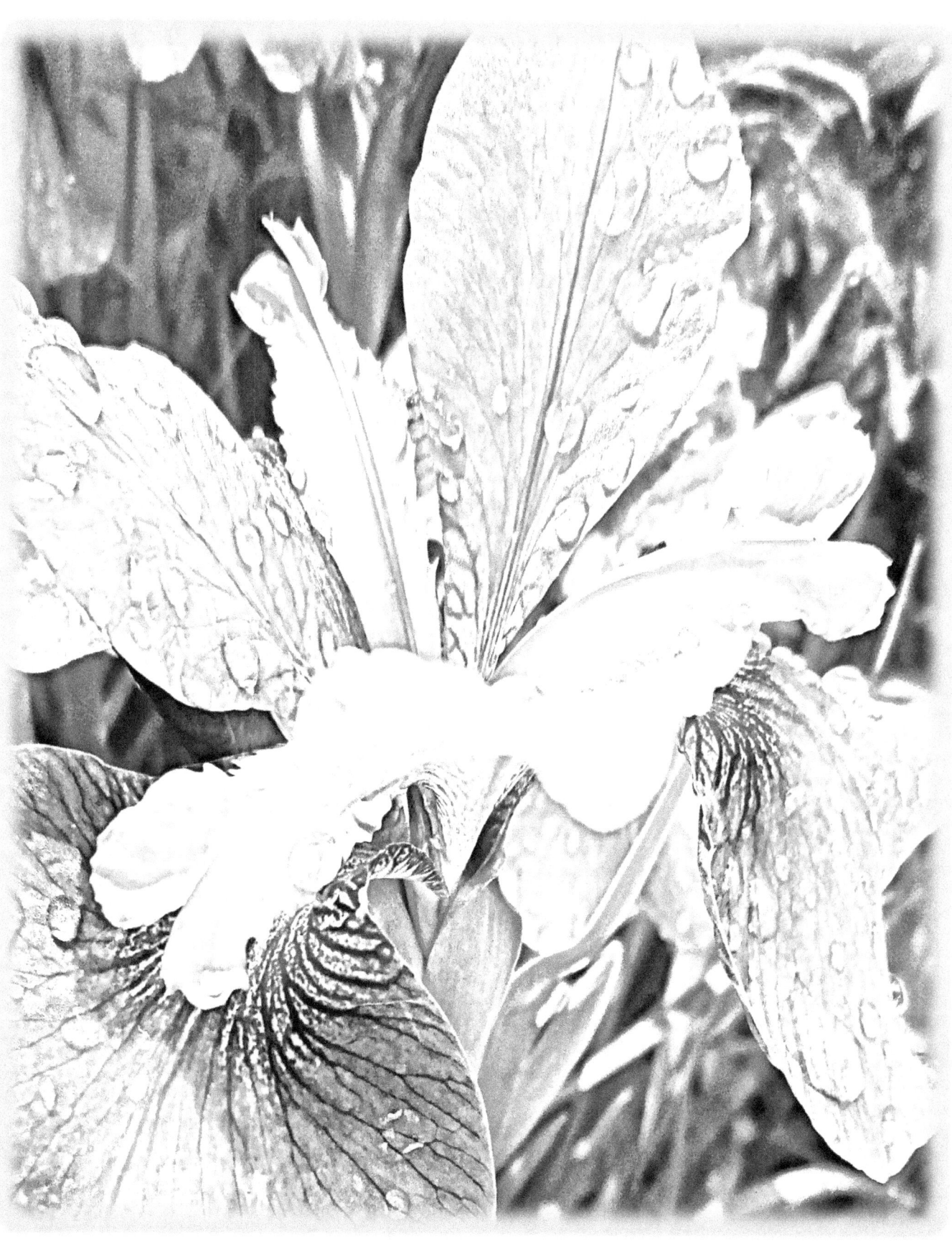

~ Siberian Iris ~

ETSY https://www.janetlongarts/shop/Etsy.com

WEBSITE [under construction] www.janetlongarts.com

The right to reproduce does not transfer with sale of artwork.

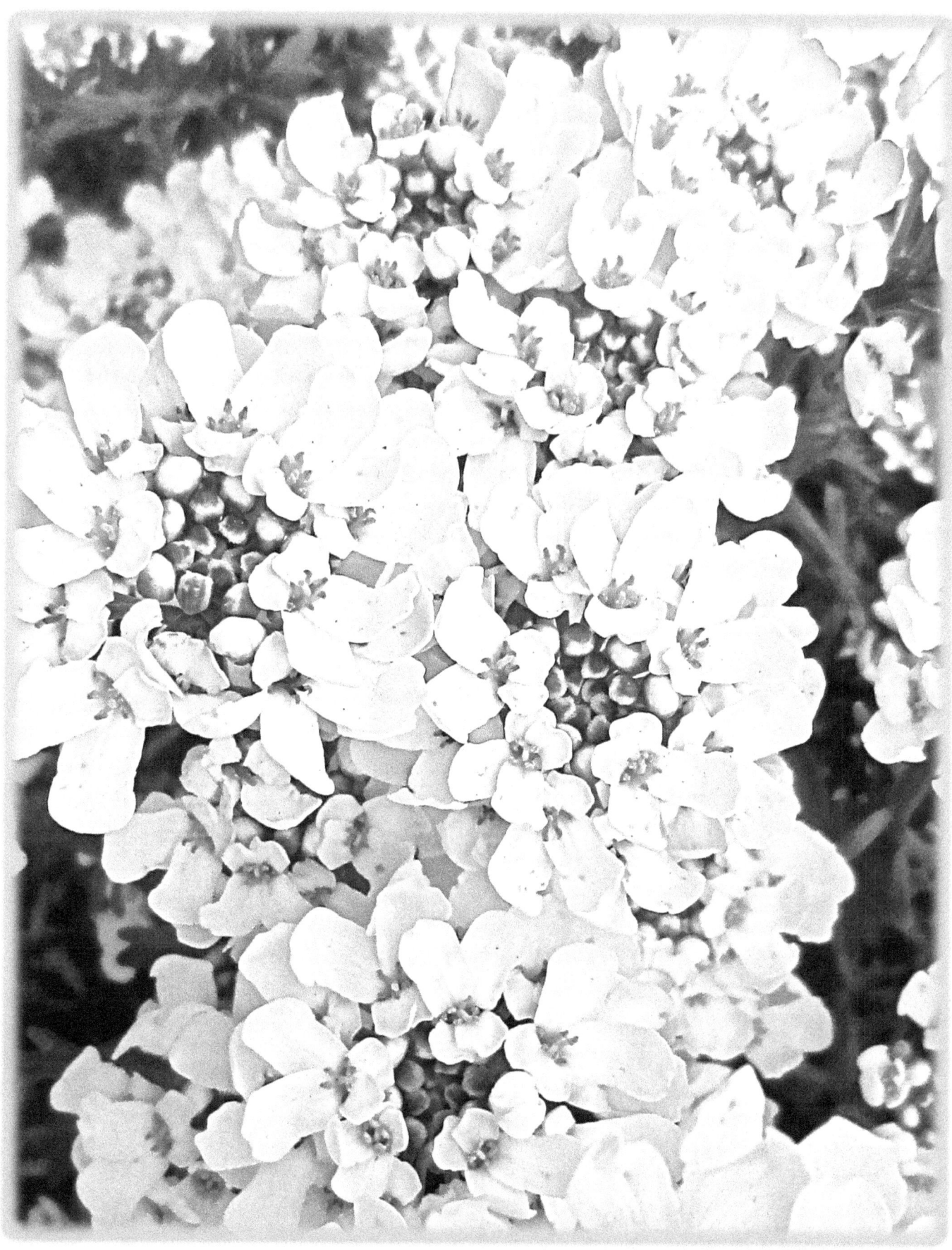

~ Candy Tuft ~

ETSY https://www.janetlongarts/shop/Etsy.com

WEBSITE [under construction] www.janetlongarts.com

The right to reproduce does not transfer with sale of artwork.

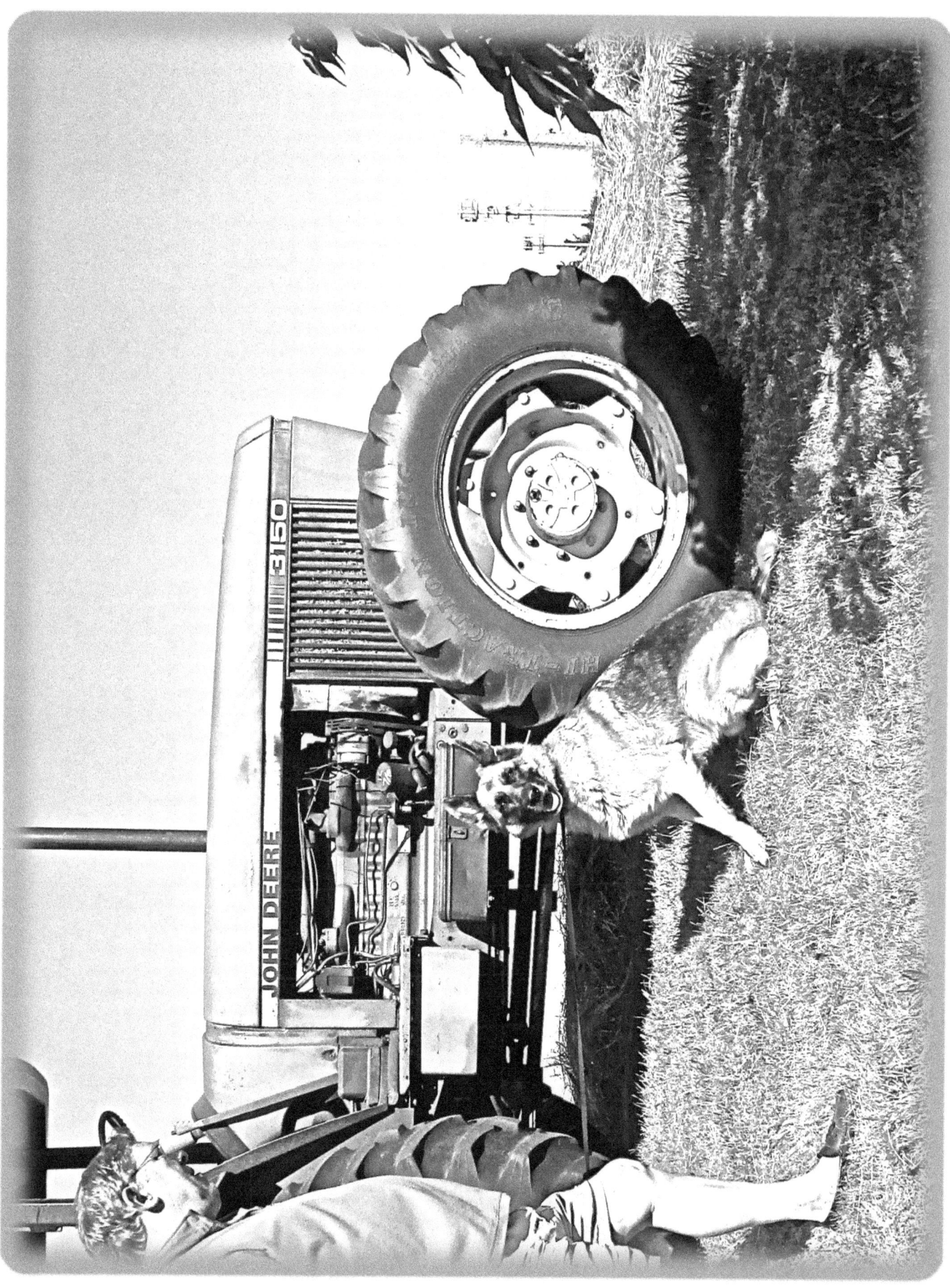

Farmer, Tractor & Koenig

our beloved German Shepherd went to Heaven in May 2015 ~
ETSY https://www.janetlongarts/shop/Etsy.com
WEBSITE [under construction] www.janetlongarts.com
The right to reproduce does not transfer with sale of artwork.

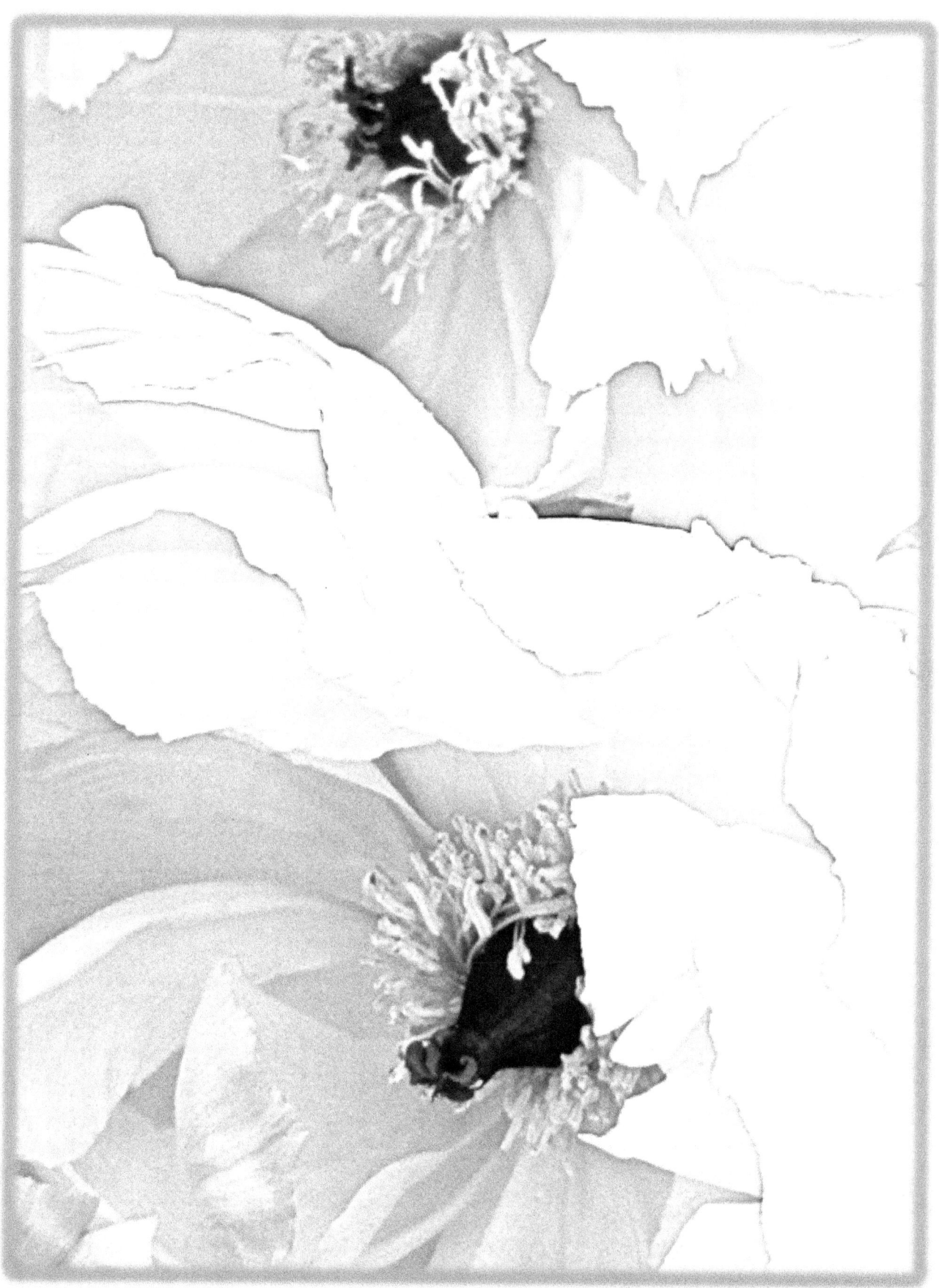

~ *Pink Peony Twins a tree peony* ~

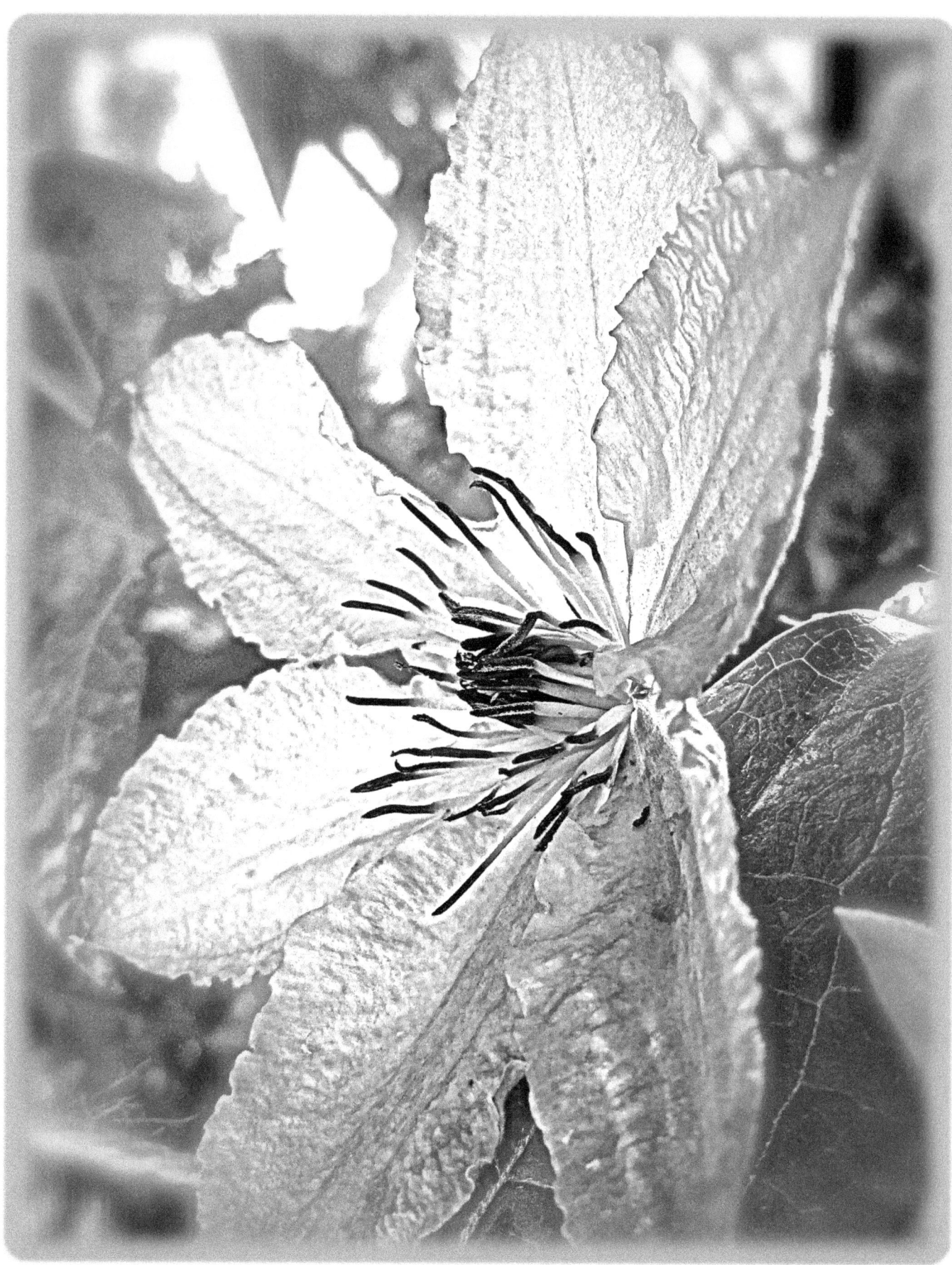

~ "Twilight" Clematis ~

ETSY https://www.janetlongarts/shop/Etsy.com

WEBSITE [under construction] www.janetlongarts.com

The right to reproduce does not transfer with sale of artwork.

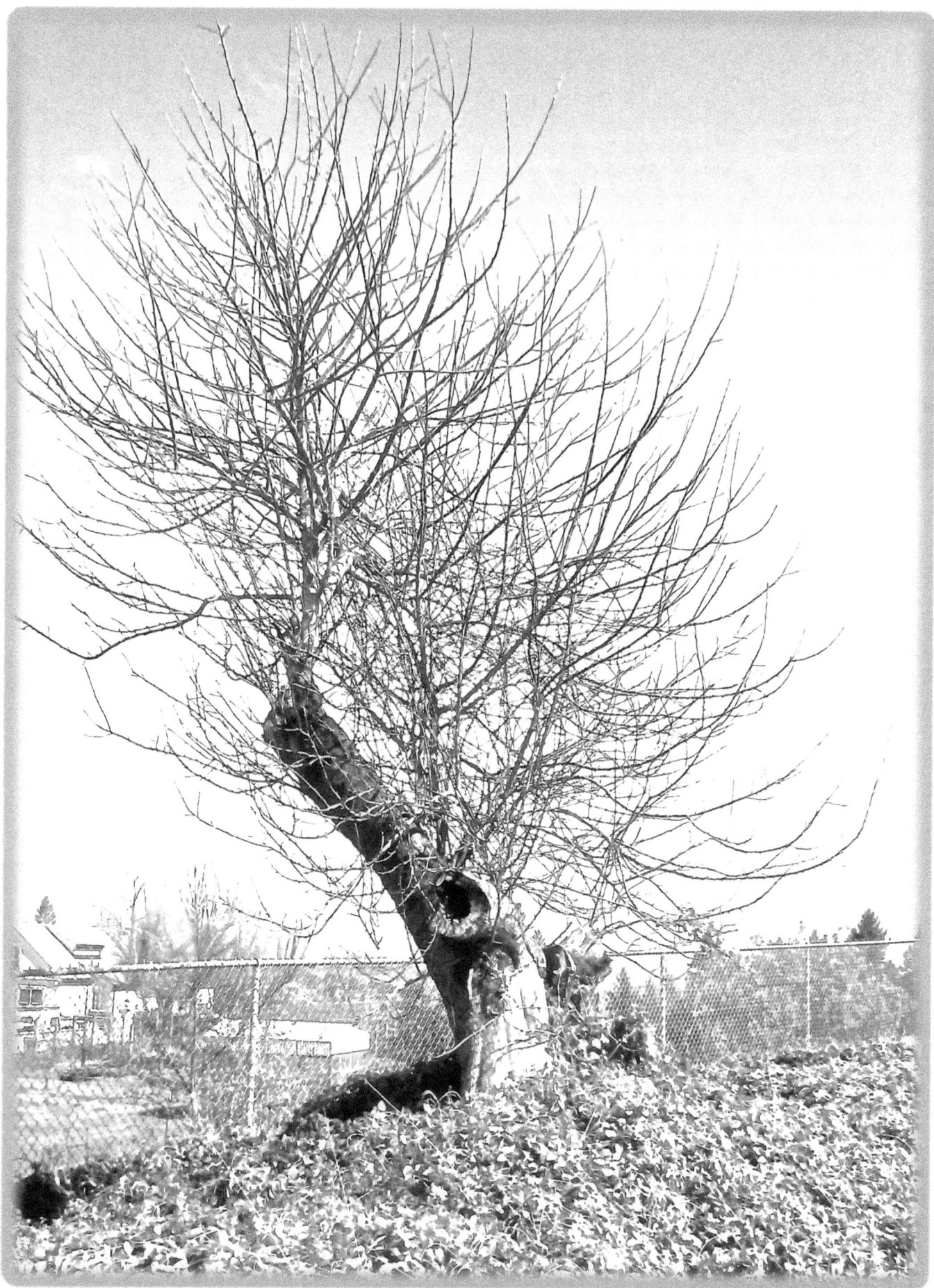

~ Old Apple Tree ~

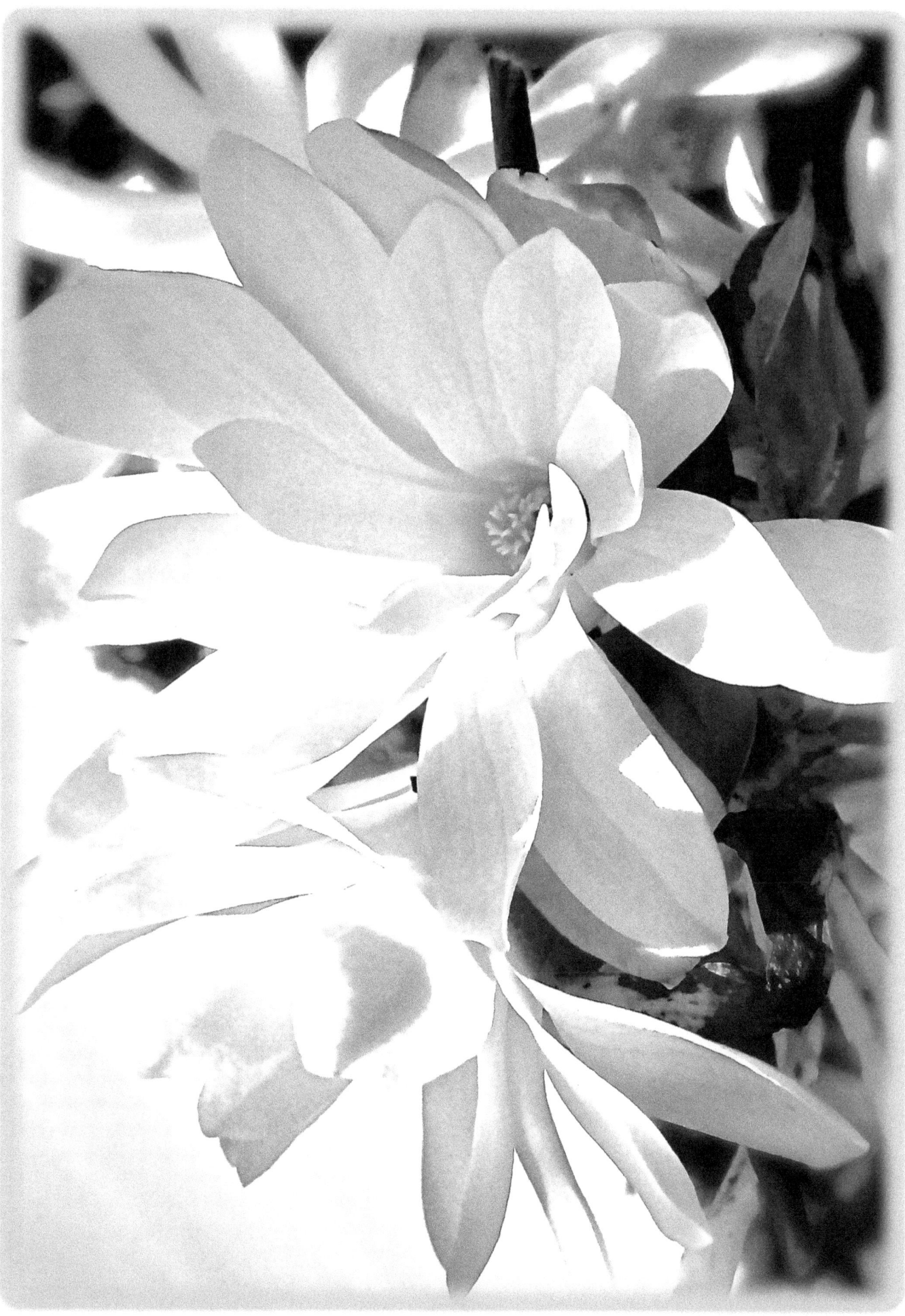

~ *Magnolia Stellata* ~

ETSY https://www.janetlongarts/shop/Etsy.com

WEBSITE [under construction] www.janetlongarts.com

The right to reproduce does not transfer with sale of artwork.

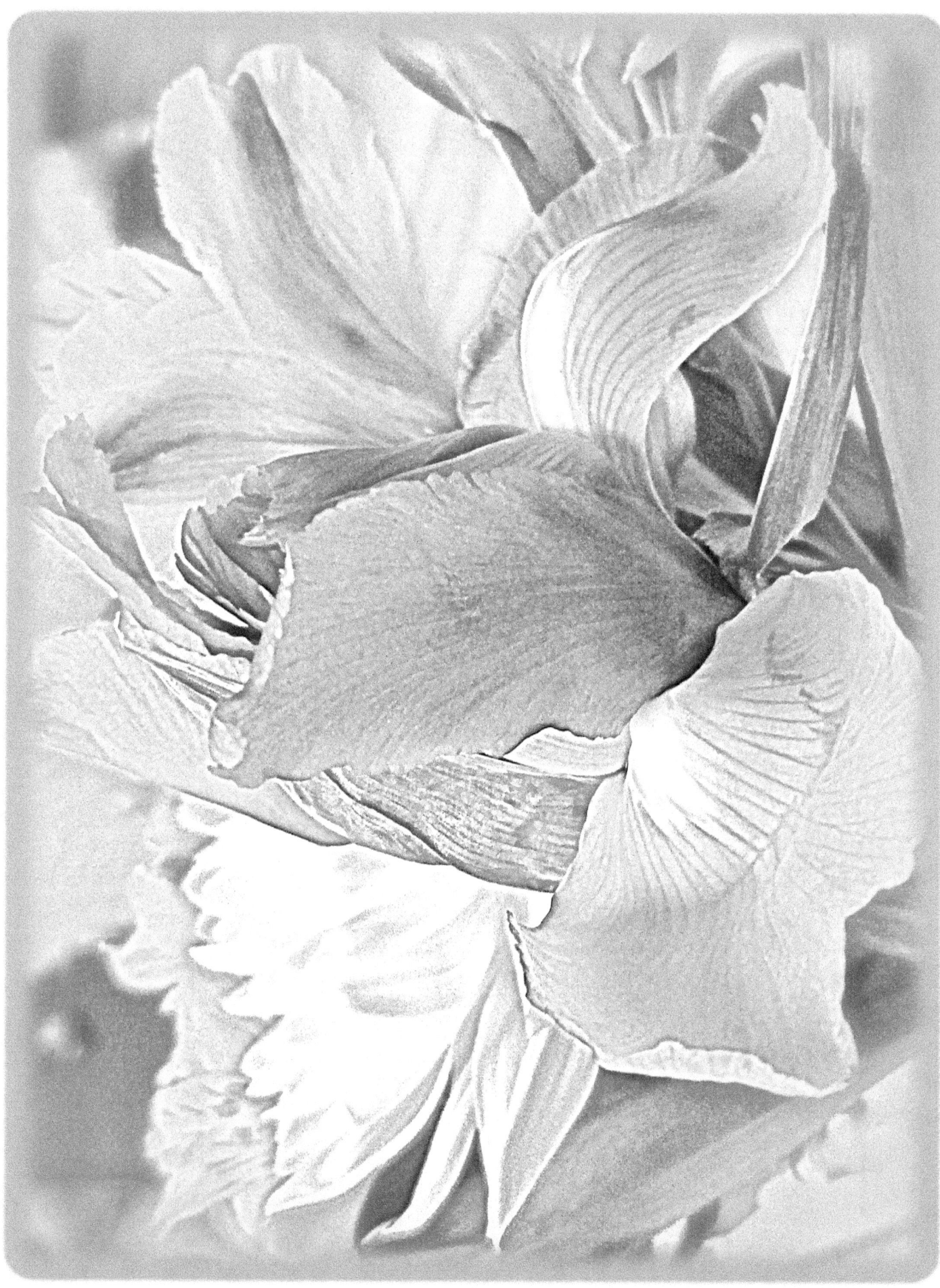

~ Iris Bouquet ~

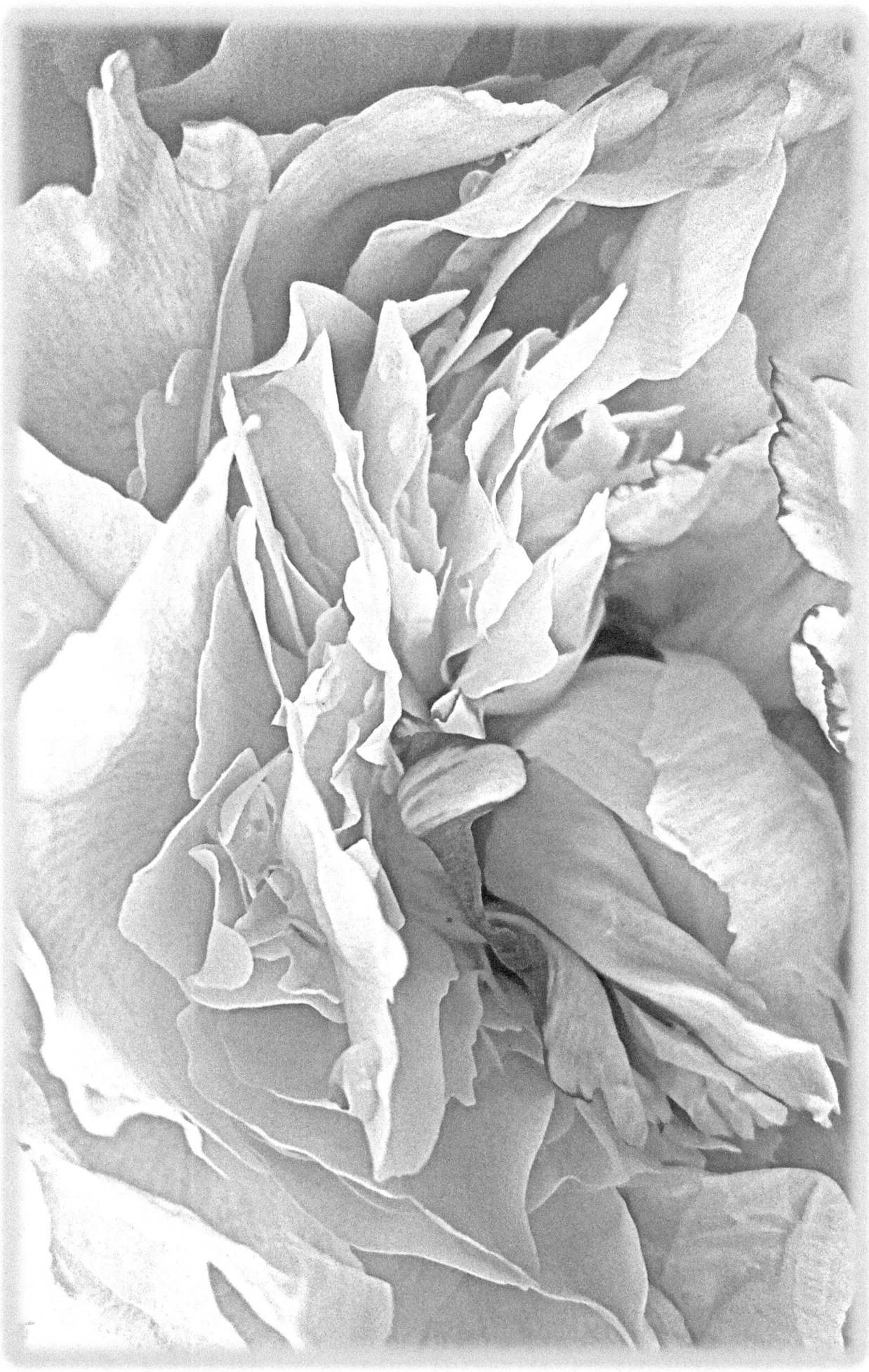

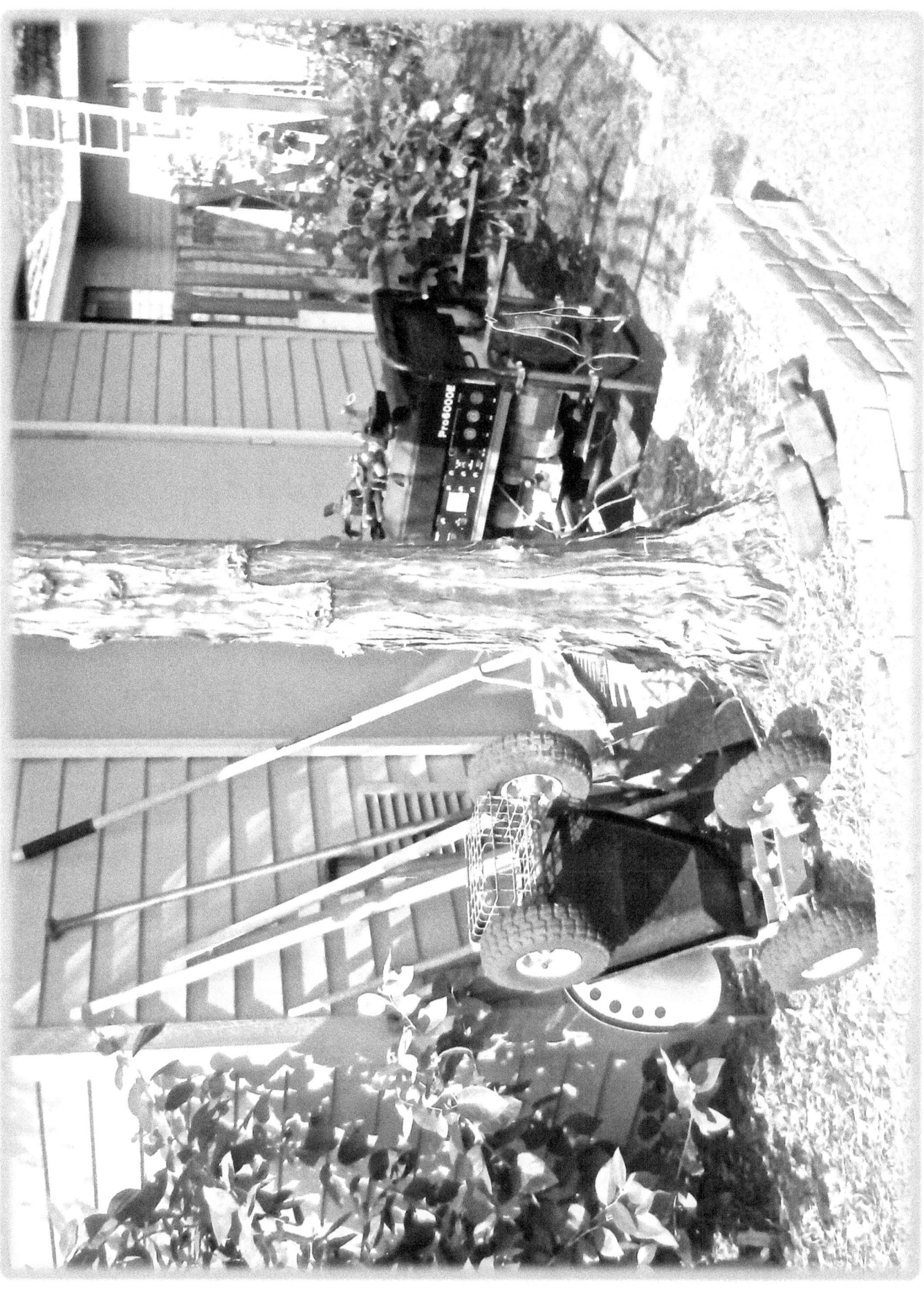

~ Garden Tools ~

ETSY https://www.janetlongarts/shop/Etsy.com
WEBSITE [under construction] www.janetlongarts.com

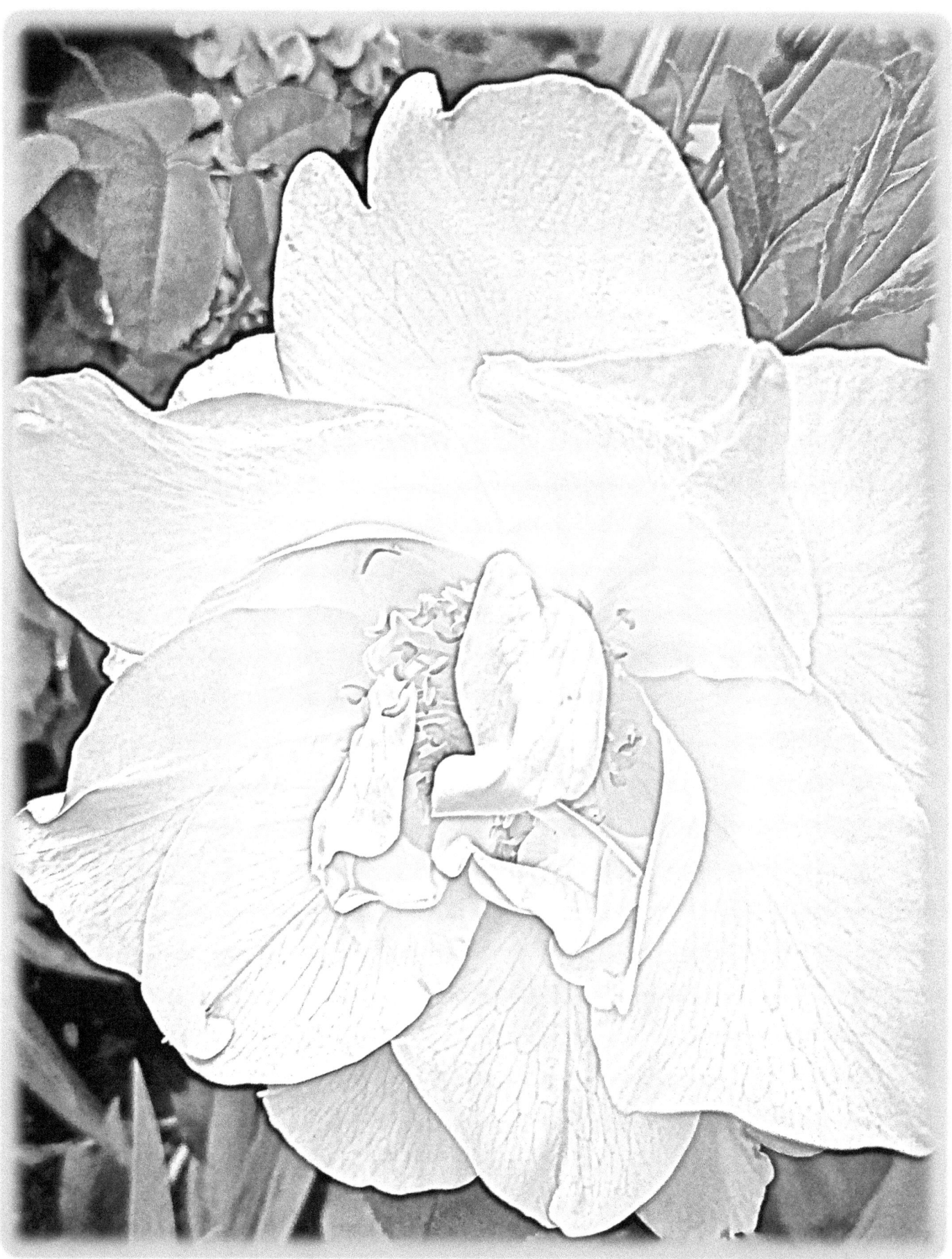

~ *"Windrush" Rose* ~

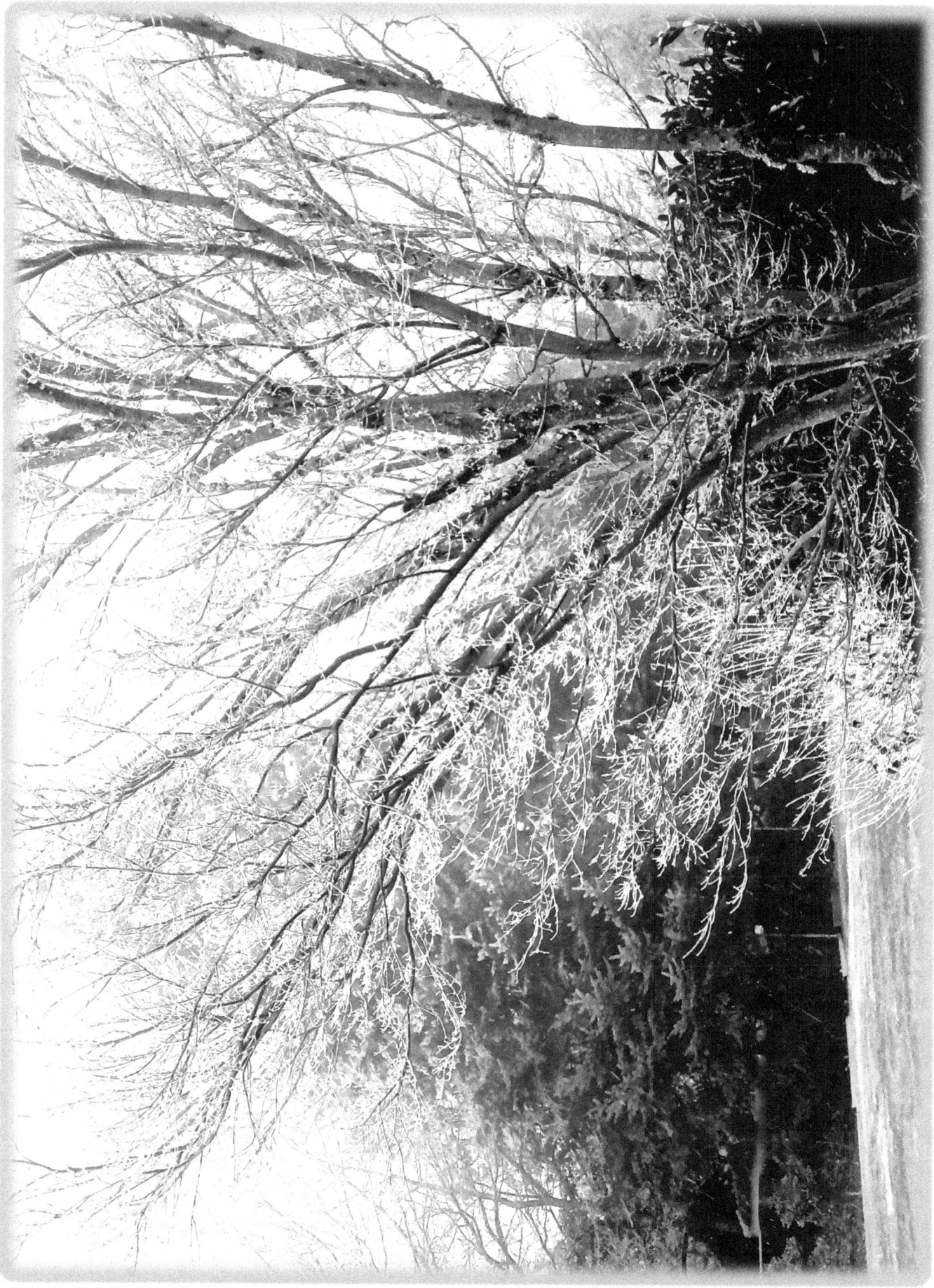

~ Frosted Tree ~

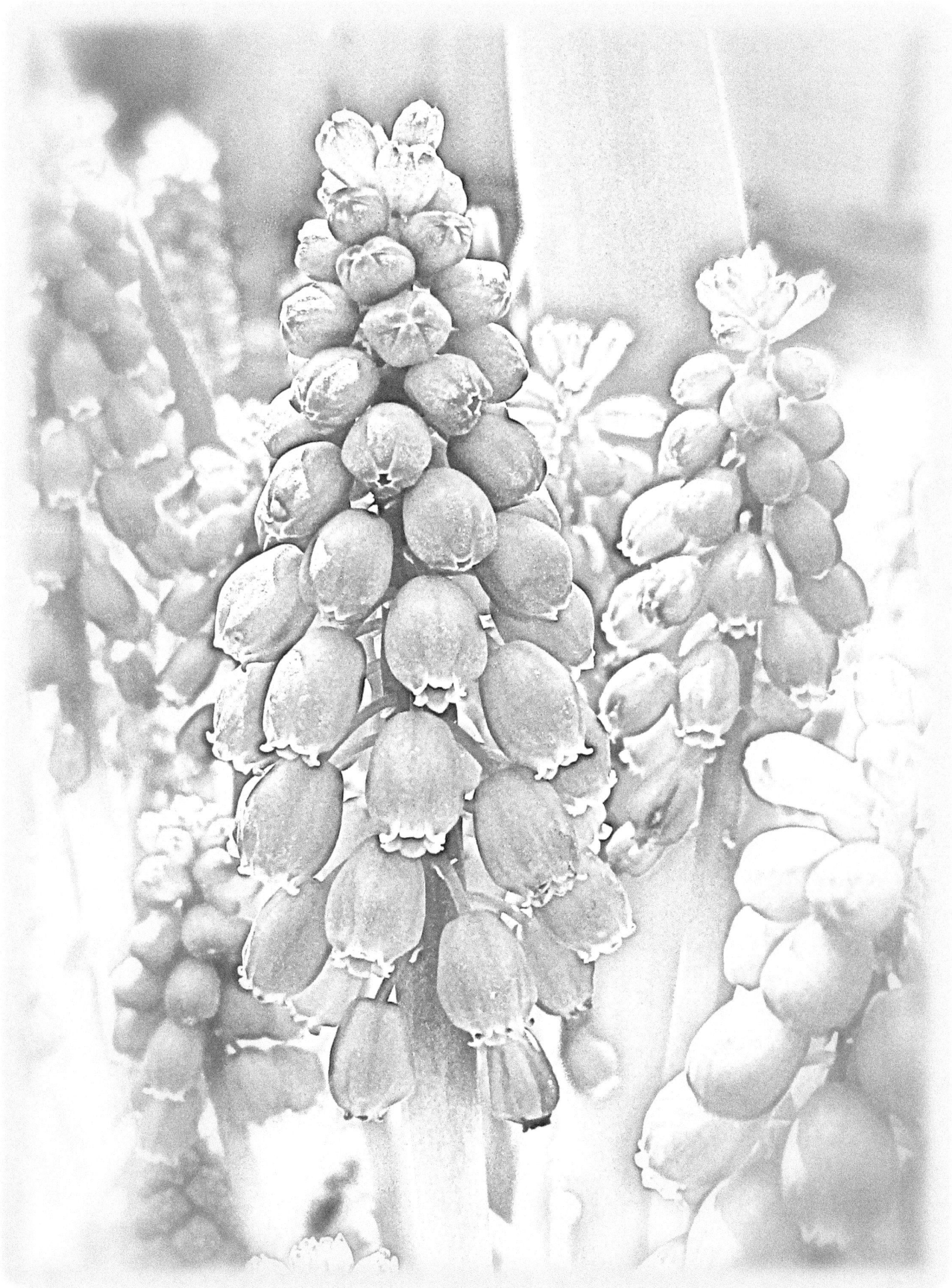

"Grape Hyacinth"

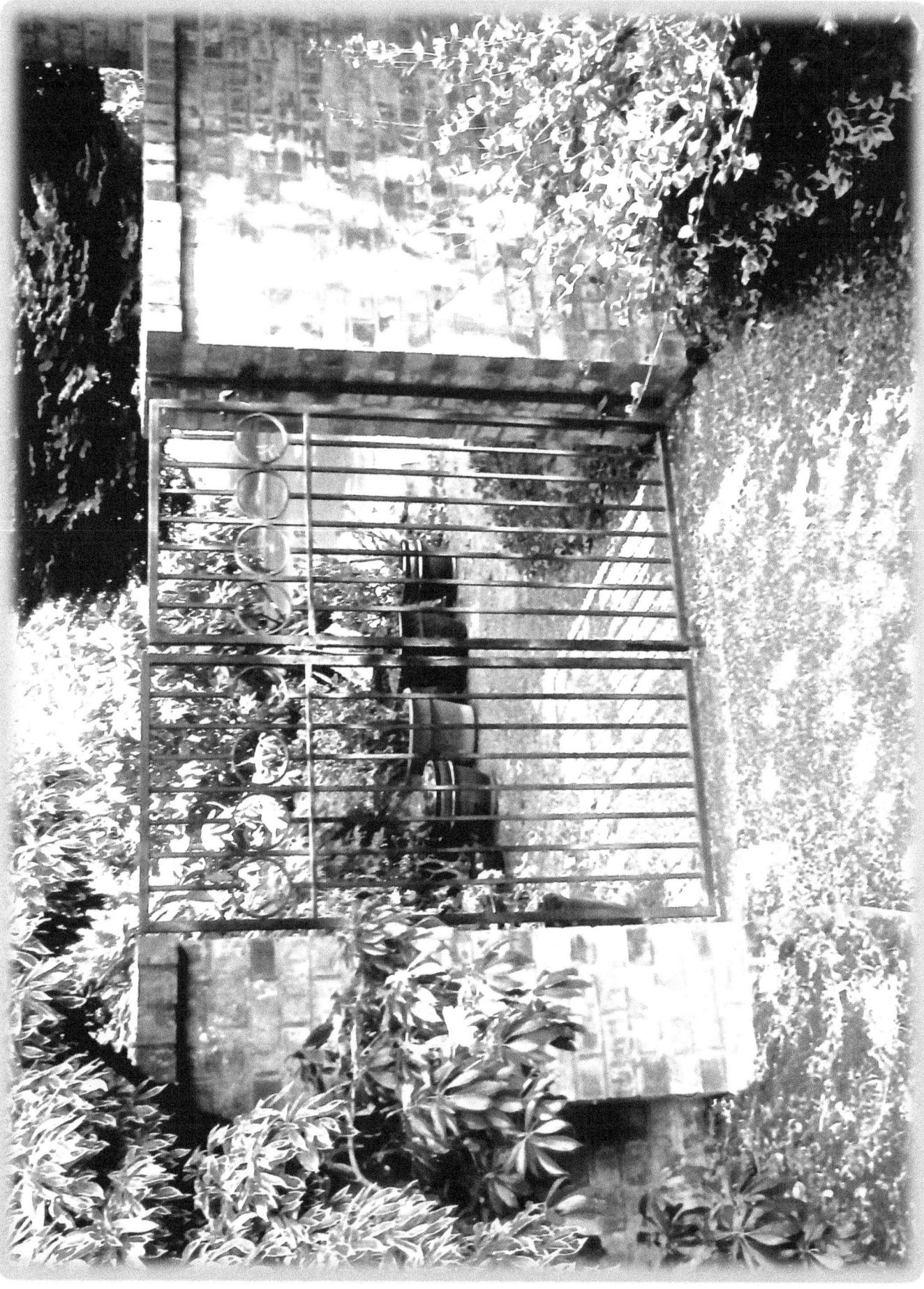

~ Back Garden Gate ~

ETSY https://www.janetlongarts/shop/Etsy.com

WEBSITE [under construction] www.janetlongarts.com

www.ingramcontent.com/pod-product-compliance
Lightning Source LLC
Chambersburg PA
CBHW080548190526

45169CB00007B/2683